KT-177-028

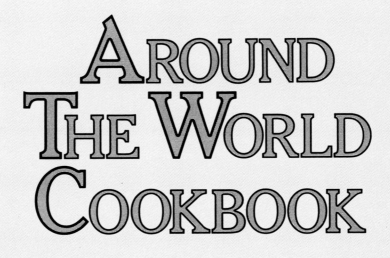

# AROUND THE WORLD COOKBOOK

Marshall Cavendish

*Editor* Emma Johnson
*Designers* Mike and Sue Rose

Published by Marshall Cavendish Limited
58 Old Compton Street
London W1V 5PA

© Marshall Cavendish Limited 1985
ISBN 0 86307 368 9
Printed in Hong Kong by Dai Nippon

# INTRODUCTION

The different cuisines of the world offer new and exciting dishes, yet many cooks are deterred from trying them because of the unfamiliar ingredients and techniques involved. All the dishes in this collection have an authentic feel, yet they are made with readily available ingredients that can be bought at large supermarkets, health food stores or ethnic food shops.

With this book as a guide, you can explore a wide variety of culinary styles and learn about the traditions and customs associated with each national dish. The result will be meals that delight your family and friends, and make you a successful international cook. Try stir-fried Chinese vegetables, accompanied by spicy sauces, Australian barbecue food, nourishing soups and stews or festive cakes and biscuits from Austria and Germany. Plan a complete Indian main course with a colourful Madras curry or a delicate chicken korma, garnished with hot pickle and served with rice and poppadoms. Whatever the occasion — a dinner party, informal supper or light summer lunch — there is an unusual dish here to make it extra special.

## SYMBOLS

**FREEZING**
When to freeze a dish

**WATCHPOINT**
Pitfalls to avoid during preparation

**TIME**
1-2 hours

**TIME**
Over 2 hours

**TIME TRAP**
Allow extra time

# CONTENTS

# FRANCE

Not surprisingly, *Coq au vin* (chicken in wine) originated in Burgundy, one of the great wine-growing districts of France. The chicken is cooked with tiny onions and mushrooms in a sauce containing brandy as well as red wine. *Coq au vin* is one of the glories of French provincial cooking and features widely on menus throughout France – from the smartest restaurant to the most homely bistro.

## Coq au vin

**SERVES 4**

1.5 kg/3-3½ lb oven-ready chicken, jointed into 8 pieces (see Cook's tip)
2 tablespoons plain flour
salt and freshly ground black pepper
75 g/3 oz butter
250 g/9 oz streaky bacon rashers, rinds removed and diced
8 button onions
2 cloves garlic, crushed
250 g/9 oz button mushrooms
2 tablespoons brandy
450 ml/16 fl oz robust red wine
225 ml/8 fl oz strong chicken stock
bouquet garni

**BEURRE MANIE (kneaded butter)**
1 tablespoon plain flour
15 g/½ oz butter

1 Put the flour in a large polythene bag and season with 1 teaspoon salt and ¼ teaspoon pepper. Add the chicken pieces and shake to coat the chicken thoroughly.
2 Melt 50 g/2 oz of the butter in a large flameproof casserole or saucepan, add the diced bacon and fry over moderate heat, stirring occasionally, for about 5 minutes until golden brown. Remove the bacon from the casserole with a slotted spoon and reserve.
3 Add the onions and garlic to the fat in the casserole and fry gently, stirring occasionally, for about 5 minutes, until golden brown. Add mushrooms and fry, stirring, for 1 minute. Remove vegetables from the casserole with a slotted spoon and reserve with the bacon.
4 Melt the remaining butter in the casserole, add the floured chicken

pieces and fry over moderate heat, turning, for 3-4 minutes until browned on all sides. Remove the chicken pieces from the heat.
5 Warm the brandy in a small saucepan and pour over the chicken. Ignite immediately with a match, shaking the casserole once or twice until the flames die down.
6 Return the reserved vegetables and bacon to the casserole, pour in the wine and stock and add the bouquet garni. Bring to the boil, stirring, then cover and simmer gently for 30-40 minutes, or until the chicken is tender and cooked through (the juices run clear when the flesh is pierced in the thickest part with a fine skewer).
7 Meanwhile, heat the oven to 110C/225F/Gas ¼. Make the beurre

manié: blend the flour and butter together with a palette knife to make a smooth paste, then cut the paste into pea-sized pieces.
8 When the chicken pieces are cooked, transfer them with a slotted spoon to a plate and keep warm in the oven. Remove the onions and mushrooms in the same way and keep warm with the chicken. Discard the bouquet garni.
9 Whisk the pieces of beurre manié into the sauce in the casserole. Simmer over low heat, whisking constantly, until the sauce thickens.
10 Simmer for 1-2 minutes, then return the chicken, onions and mushrooms to the casserole and turn to coat in the sauce. Serve at once, straight from the casserole (see Serving ideas).

## Cook's Notes

**TIME**
Preparation, including pre-cooking, takes about 20 minutes. Cooking, including thickening the sauce, takes about 40 minutes.

**COOK'S TIP**
To enrich the flavour of the dish even further, marinate the chicken pieces overnight in the wine, then drain and pat dry with absorbent paper before coating with the seasoned flour.

**SERVING IDEAS**
Serve with buttered rice with chives (*riz à la ciboulette*), slices of French bread and a leafy green salad preferably made with endive, a favourite French salad vegetable, tossed in an oil and vinegar dressing.

**DID YOU KNOW**
French cooks sometimes thicken the sauce with the pounded liver of the chicken. A farmer's wife drawing her own chicken would mix some of the blood with the chicken liver.

**FREEZING**
Cool quickly, then transfer to a rigid container, seal, label and freeze for up to 3 months. To serve: defrost overnight in the refrigerator, transfer to a large saucepan and bring slowly to the boil over gentle heat, stirring frequently. Simmer for at least 5 minutes, then taste and adjust seasoning if necessary before transferring the chicken to a warmed serving dish.

●1065 calories/4450 kj per portion

**Sole Véronique is a classic French dish of lightly poached fillets of sole served in a creamy white wine sauce, garnished with tiny green grapes. The colour of the dish is subtly pale and the flavour is delicate, the grapes giving a juicy texture that complements the softness of the fish. It makes a perfect main course for a summer dinner party.**

The name Véronique was originally given to this dish by Monsieur Malley, head chef at the Ritz hotel in London at the turn of the century. Monsieur Malley decided to add grapes to the white wine sauce in a fish dish he was preparing for a party at the hotel. The dish was named after the baby girl born to his assistant chef on the day of the party, and since then the term (Véronique) has been used to describe any savoury dish cooked with white wine and grapes.

single layer, skinned side downwards, in an ovenproof dish. Tuck both ends of each fillet under, so that the fillets are all the same length.

**5** Pour over enough of the reduced fish stock just to cover the fish. Cover the dish with a lid or foil and cook in the oven for 15 minutes.

**6** Meanwhile, plunge the grapes into boiling water for 5 seconds, drain and remove skins.

**7** When the fish is cooked, turn the oven down to 140C/275F/Gas 1. Carefully remove the poached fillets from the baking dish, place them on an ovenproof plate with the grapes and keep warm in the oven. [!] Strain the cooking liquid into a clean saucepan and boil vigorously to

reduce by half. Measure out 150 ml/ ¼ pint into a measuring jug.

**8** To make the sauce: melt the butter in a saucepan, sprinkle in the flour and stir over low heat for 1-2 minutes until straw-coloured. Remove from the heat and gradually stir in the milk and the 150 ml/¼ pint reduced cooking liquid. Return to the heat and bring to the boil, stirring constantly. Reduce the heat and simmer for 2 minutes, until thickened and smooth. Remove from the heat and stir in the cream and half the grapes with salt and pepper to taste.

**9** Arrange the fillets of sole on a warmed flat serving dish. Pour the sauce evenly over the fish and scatter the remaining grapes on top.

## Sole Véronique

**SERVES 4**

3 × 350 g/12 oz sole, skinned and each cut into 4 fillets, bones and trimmings reserved (see Buying guide)
10 black peppercorns
1 onion, sliced
1 celery stalk, sliced
1 bay leaf
150 ml/¼ pint dry white wine
100 g/4 oz seedless green grapes (see Buying guide)
25 g/1 oz butter
25 g/1 oz plain flour
300 ml/½ pint milk
4 tablespoons double cream
salt and freshly ground white pepper

**1** Make the stock: place the fish bones and trimmings in a large saucepan. Add the peppercorns, onion, celery, bay leaf and white wine, and pour in just enough fresh cold water to cover the bones. Bring to the boil, reduce the heat and simmer for about 20 minutes. [!]

**2** Strain the fish stock into a clean saucepan and boil to reduce by half.

**3** Heat the oven to 180C/350F/Gas 4.

**4** Trim any untidy edges from the fish fillets, then place them in a

# Cook's Notes

### TIME
Preparation, including making the stock and sauce, takes about 1 hour. Cooking the fish in the oven takes 15 minutes.

### BUYING GUIDE
Dover sole has a particularly fine texture, but is very expensive. Lemon sole is cheaper, and can be used as a substitute, if wished. If your fishmonger is filleting the fish for you, remember to ask him to give you the bones and trimmings for stock.

The best grapes to use are either Sultana grapes from Cyprus (available July and August), or Thomas grapes from Chile (available January-April). Both these types are tiny and seedless. If neither is available, use ordinary green grapes: cut them in half, if liked, and then remove the seeds after peeling the grapes.

### VARIATION
Fresh sole is preferable, but you can also use frozen fillets. In this case, do not make the fish stock as described in stage 1: just place the defrosted fillets in an ovenproof dish, add the peppercorns, sliced onion and celery, bay leaf and 150 ml/¼ pint white wine and fresh cold water just to cover. Cover the dish and cook in the oven for 15 minutes. Continue from stage 6 and in stage 7 measure out 150 ml/¼ pint cooking liquid to make the sauce. The result will be good, but the sauce will not be quite so thick and flavoursome: a perfect sauce needs to be made with a twice-reduced fish stock.

### COOK'S TIP
To remove the fishy smell from the saucepans used for the stock, soak the pans in water with a little mustard powder dissolved in it.

### WATCHPOINTS
When making fish stock, never simmer the bones for longer than 25 minutes, or the stock tends to become bitter.

It is important to warm the grapes through thoroughly in the oven. However, fish tends to overcook easily, and should not be kept warm for too long. Try not to leave it in the oven for more than 10 minutes. Have everything ready to make the sauce, to ensure that there are no unnecessary delays.

### SERVING IDEAS
Serve a crisp green vegetable to complement the softness of the fish fillets. Lightly cooked broccoli or courgettes would be ideal. Plainly boiled or steamed tiny new potatoes are also a good accompaniment.

●325 calories/1375 kj per portion

The true king of casseroles, Boeuf à la bourguignonne gets both its name and its wonderful mellow richness from the full-bodied red Burgundy wine in which it is first marinated and then slowly simmered. Much of the world's most famous food and wine comes from this region, which stretches southeast of Paris up to the Swiss border.

The secret of making a Boeuf à la bourguignonne, that would do a Burgundian chef credit, lies not in elaborate cooking methods but in carefully chosen ingredients, plenty of time for marinating and long, gentle cooking. So choose good-quality meat, a true Burgundy wine such as Côte de Beaune, Savigny or Pommard, and do not try to rush the simmering process.

To serve Boeuf à la bourguignonne in true French style, accompany it simply with plenty of fresh crusty bread and tossed green salad. Drink a red Burgundy wine to make it a French meal to remember.

## Boeuf à la bourguignonne

SERVES 4

1 kg/2 lb chuck steak, cut into large pieces 10 cm/4 inches long
2-3 tablespoons olive oil
175 g/6 oz unsmoked streaky bacon, preferably in 1 piece, diced
2 medium onions, sliced
2 medium carrots, sliced
2 tablespoons plain flour
salt and freshly ground black pepper
3 tablespoons brandy (optional)
1 large clove garlic, crushed
bouquet garni (parsley, thyme, bay leaf)
about 150 ml/¼ pint boiling water

MARINADE
300 ml/½ pint red Burgundy wine
2 tablespoons olive oil
½ teaspoon dried mixed herbs

TO FINISH
25 g/1 oz butter
250 g/9 oz whole button onions
250 g/9 oz button mushrooms
75 ml/3 fl oz red wine
1 teaspoon brown sugar

1 Place the chuck steak in a shallow dish. Add the marinade ingredients and turn the meat in them several times. Cover and leave in a cool place for at least 3 hours, turning the meat occasionally.
2 Heat the oven to 180C/350F/Gas 4.
3 Heat 2 tablespoons olive oil in a large frying-pan over moderate heat, add the bacon and fry until golden brown. Remove with slotted spoon, drain on absorbent paper.
4 Turn the heat down to low, add the sliced onions and carrots and fry for about 15 minutes until the onions are golden. Remove with a slotted spoon and drain on the paper with the bacon.
5 Remove the meat from the marinade and drain thoroughly in a sieve, making sure you save all the liquid. Pat the meat dry with absorbent paper.
6 Add another tablespoon olive oil to the frying-pan if needed. Increase the heat and fry the meat briskly until brown on all sides.
7 Season the flour with salt and pepper, then sprinkle over the meat. Fry the meat for another 5 minutes, turning it constantly. Stir in the reserved marinade and the brandy (if using) and bring to the boil, scraping up all the sediment from the sides and bottom of the pan.
8 Transfer the meat and marinade to a flameproof casserole. Add the reserved bacon, onions and carrots with the garlic and bouquet garni, then pour in enough boiling water just to cover the meat and vegetables. Bring to the boil, then cover the casserole and transfer it to the oven. Cook for 2 hours or until the meat is tender but still firm. Check the contents of the casserole occasionally and add a little more boiling water if too dry.
9 To finish: melt the butter in a frying-pan over moderate heat. Add the whole button onions and mushrooms and fry for 2-3 minutes.

Pour in the wine, stir in the sugar and bring to the boil. Stir this mixture into the casserole, replace the lid and continue cooking for a further 30 minutes until the meat and onions are tender.
10 Skim off any excess fat from the casserole with a skimmer or slotted spoon. Discard the bouquet garni, then taste and adjust seasoning. Serve hot, straight from casserole.

## Cook's Notes

TIME
Preparation takes about 45 minutes, cooking 2½ hours, but remember that the meat needs at least 3 hours marinating time.

BUYING GUIDE
It is worth the extra expense of using olive oil and butter to make this dish – substitutes will not give a perfect flavour. Similarly, select a true full-bodied Burgundy for the marinade. A miniature bottle of brandy will supply the 3 tablespoons you need to make this dish.
If you cannot find button onions (also called pickling onions), buy shallots instead.

WATCHPOINT
The meat must be thoroughly dry before it is fried or it will not brown.

FREEZING
Pack into one or more rigid containers, seal, label and freeze for up to 6 months. To serve: reheat from frozen over low heat until bubbling.

●920 calories/3850 kj per portion

Profiteroles — little choux pastry buns — make an impressive-looking dessert. The pastry swells into crisp, hollow shells which, in France, are traditionally filled with sweetened whipped cream. Other more unusual fillings can be used, such as the ice cream in this recipe. For maximum impact, pile the profiteroles high and pour chocolate sauce over them.

# Profiteroles

**MAKES 22**

130 g/4½ oz strong plain flour (see
   Watchpoints)
2 teaspoons caster sugar
250 ml/9 fl oz water
100 g/4 oz slightly salted butter, cut
   into small pieces
4 eggs
1 teaspoon brandy, rum or orange
   flower water (optional)
   1 litre/2.2 pints vanilla ice
   cream (see Cook's tip)
beaten egg and sugar, to glaze

CHOCOLATE SAUCE
250 g/9 oz plain dessert chocolate
175 ml/6 fl oz milk
piece of vanilla pod
2 tablespoons double cream
40 g/1½ oz butter
115 g/4 oz sugar

**1** Heat the oven to 200C/400F/Gas 6.
**2** Sift the flour and sugar twice, then sift on to a sheet of greaseproof paper. Set aside.
**3** Put water into a deep saucepan and add the butter. Place the pan over low heat and warm gently until all the butter has melted, then increase the heat to bring the liquid to a rolling boil. Draw the pan aside immediately and shoot in the flour mixture all at once. Lower the heat and return the pan to the cooker immediately then, using a large wooden spoon, beat the paste vigorously until the flour has cooked and the mixture is smooth. It must not look grainy and should roll cleanly off the sides of the pan into a ball, leaving a floury film over the base. [!] Remove from the heat and leave to cool in the saucepan for about 5 minutes.
**4** Break 1 egg into a cup and beat lightly with a fork, then pour on to the flour paste and beat thoroughly to blend. Continue in the same way with the remaining eggs, adding only a little at a time towards the end, so the mixture does not get too moist (you may even need a little more egg if conditions are very dry). [!] The finished paste should be quite firm but elastic – it will drop from a spoon slowly when

jerked. Beat the paste well until it is shiny and smooth. Beat in brandy, rum or orange flower water if using.
**5** Chill a flat baking sheet: hold it under cold running water for a few moments, shake off excess moisture but leave damp. Place teaspoonfuls of the mixture, about 2.5 cm/1 inch in size, at 5 cm/2 inch intervals on the wet sheet; leaving these large spaces to allow the profiteroles room to expand. Lightly brush a little beaten egg on each one and sprinkle over a pinch of sugar.
**6** Place sheet in the oven [!] and bake for about 20 minutes until the profiteroles are well browned all over and feel very light and hollow when picked up. [!]
**7** Remove the sheet from the oven. Pierce each bun with a skewer or knife to release the steam inside. Leave to cool on a wire rack.
**8** Meanwhile, make chocolate sauce: break the chocolate into pieces and place in a heatproof bowl over a pan a quarter full of gently simmering water (the water must not touch the bowl). Heat gently until the chocolate has melted.
**9** Pour the milk into a separate saucepan and add the vanilla pod. Bring to boiling point, then add the cream and bring back to the boil. Lift the pan off the heat, remove the vanilla pod, then stir in the melted chocolate, butter and sugar. Return to the heat and boil for a few seconds, stirring until thickened.
**10** Cut each profiterole in half. Cut the ice cream into 22 small cubes and put 1 cube into each profiterole (see Cook's tip). Pile profiteroles attractively on to a glass or china serving plate. Pour over the hot chocolate sauce and serve at once.

## Cook's Notes

### TIME
Preparing and baking the choux pastry takes 40 minutes; allow 30 minutes for cooling, during which time the chocolate sauce can be made. Allow 5 minutes for assembly.

### WATCHPOINTS
Use strong plain flour if possible, as it has a higher gluten content than ordinary plain flour, giving more volume and crispness.

The pastry mixture only takes a few seconds to cook before it forms into a ball. If allowed to cook too long the finished profiteroles will be heavy.

If the choux mixture is too moist it will fail to rise properly and be inclined to spread.

Choux pastry buns can burn very easily so it is important that the oven temperature is correct. If your oven is inclined to overheat, use a layer of foil or slide a second baking sheet underneath for added protection while cooking.

Do not open the oven door until the buns have cooked for at least 15 minutes. If not cooked sufficiently, the delicate buns may collapse.

### COOK'S TIP
The ice cream must be as hard as possible – do not use soft-scoop ice cream.

● 205 calories/850 kj per profiterole

---

## MAKING CHOUX PASTRY

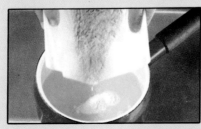

**1** Bring the water and butter to the boil. Remove from heat and shoot in the sifted flour and sugar.

**2** Scoop mixture on to a teaspoon. Using back of another spoon, push mixture on to baking sheet.

There are many delicious versions of *Tarte aux pommes*, the celebrated French apple flan. One has a creamed almond mixture the French call *frangipane* underneath the apples; another has a puréed apple base on which the apple slices are arranged. In this popular version, a cream and egg custard is poured over the apples in the rich shortcrust case.

# Tarte aux pommes

**SERVES 6**

500 g/1 lb dessert apples, peeled, cored and cut into 5 mm/¼ inch slices (see Steps and Buying guide)
50 g/2 oz unsalted butter
3 eggs
2 tablespoons caster sugar
pinch of ground cinnamon
pinch of freshly grated nutmeg
300 ml/½ pint single cream

**PASTRY**

175 g/6 oz plain flour
pinch of salt
75 g/3 oz caster sugar
50 g/2 oz unsalted butter, softened
3 large egg yolks

**GLAZE**

3 tablespoons apricot jam
2 tablespoons kirsch, Calvados or brandy

1 Make the pastry: sift the flour and salt into a bowl. Make a well in the centre and add the sugar, butter and egg yolks.
2 Using the fingertips of one hand, or a fork, gradually work the butter, sugar and egg yolks together. Gradually incorporate the flour until the dough forms a ball. Wrap in cling film and refrigerate for 30 minutes (see Cook's tips).
3 Meanwhile, make the glaze: put the jam in a small saucepan with the kirsch. Stir over gentle heat until the jam has dissolved. Sieve the mixture through a nylon sieve and set aside.
4 Heat the oven to 220C/425F/Gas 7.
5 Roll out the pastry on a lightly floured surface to a circle 2.5 cm/1 inch larger than a loose-based 25 cm/10 inch fluted flan tin. Roll the pastry circle loosely around the rolling pin, then carefully unroll it over the flan tin. ! Press the pastry into the tin, moulding it well into the fluted edge. Trim any excess pastry. Chill the lined flan tin in the refrigerator for 15-20 minutes.
6 Place a large circle of greaseproof paper or foil in the pastry case and weight it down with baking beans. Bake blind in the oven for 15 minutes, then remove from the oven and lower the oven heat to 200C/400F/Gas 6.
7 While the pastry case is baking, prepare the filling: melt the butter in a large frying-pan; add the apple slices and cook gently for 4-5 minutes until they just begin to soften, turning them carefully with a fish slice. !
8 Arrange the apple slices (see Steps and Cook's tips) in the partially-baked pastry case. Whisk together the eggs, sugar, spices and cream and pour evenly over the slices.
9 Bake the flan in the oven for 25-30 minutes until the custard is just set and firm to the touch.
10 Meanwhile, reheat the apricot glaze in a small saucepan. Bring just to boiling point.
11 Allow the apple flan to cool slightly, then brush the surface with the hot glaze. Allow to cool slightly, remove from tin and place on serving plate. Serve warm or cold.

## Cook's Notes

**TIME**
Preparing and chilling the pastry case takes about 50 minutes (make the glaze during chilling). Baking blind and preparing the filling take about 15 minutes; filling the pastry case and glazing about 30 minutes, and baking in the oven about 30 minutes.

**WATCHPOINTS**
If the pastry breaks, simply press the edges back together again.
Be careful not to overcook the apple slices or they will lose their shape and become mushy when baked.

**BUYING GUIDE**
The French often use Reinette apples in flans, a variety similar to the English Russet. Cox's Orange Pippins would also be a very suitable alternative.

**COOK'S TIPS**
Work the pastry as little as possible to prevent it from becoming sticky. It will be quite soft, and chilling helps it firm up.
The classic French way to arrange the apple slices is in a spiral, starting at the centre of the flan. But the flan also looks very pretty if the apples are arranged in circles, starting at the edge of the tin.

**FREEZING**
Open freeze the tart until solid. Remove from flan tin, cover with cling film, overwrap in foil, seal, label and freeze for up to 3 months. To serve: unwrap, replace in flan tin, and cover with foil. Bake in the oven at 200C/400F/Gas 6 for 20 minutes. Serve warm or cold.

●455 calories/1920 kj per portion

## PREPARING AND ARRANGING APPLES

Cut apples in half, cut out core with a small sharp knife.

Peel the apples, then cut lengthways into thick slices.

Starting at centre of flan, arrange slices overlapping in a spiral shape.

Regal enough for any occasion, crown roast of lamb was a popular Edwardian dinner-party dish and is still one of the easiest and most decorative ways of serving a set number of people.

Allow each person 2 cutlets when buying the joints and you know in advance how many guests to ask!

The traditional apricot stuffing has an unusual spicy yet mild flavouring of coriander—a spice once grown in southern England and much loved in the 18th century.

## Crown roast of lamb

**SERVES 6-8**

2 best ends neck of lamb with 6-8 cutlets each, chined (see Cook's tip)
50 g/2 oz butter, melted
salt and freshly ground black pepper

**STUFFING**
15 g/½ oz butter
1 tablespoon vegetable oil
1 small onion, finely chopped
225 g/8 oz fresh white breadcrumbs
1 tablespoon coriander seeds (see Buying guide)
100 g/4 oz dried apricots, soaked overnight, then drained and roughly chopped
50 g/2 oz seedless raisins
50 g/2 oz shelled walnuts, chopped
1 tablespoon chopped parsley
beaten egg, to bind

**GRAVY**
150 ml/¼ pint chicken stock
150 ml/¼ pint dry white wine or dry cider
2 tablespoons redcurrant jelly

1 To make the stuffing: heat the butter and oil in a small saucepan. Add the onion and fry gently until soft but not browned.
2 Stir in the breadcrumbs, transfer to a bowl and leave to cool.
3 Crush the coriander seeds in a grinder or pestle and mortar, then add to the breadcrumbs with the remaining stuffing ingredients and salt and pepper to taste. Stir well to mix, then bind with beaten egg.
4 Heat the oven to 200C/400F/Gas 6.
5 To prepare the meat: see Preparation, or ask your butcher to make up the crown roast beforehand.
6 Stand the joint in a roasting tin. Season the melted butter with salt

and freshly ground black pepper and brush about half on the outside of the joint. Pour the rest into the roasting tin.

**7** Fill the centre of the joint with the stuffing and cover the top and each protruding bone end with foil.

**8** Roast the joint in the oven for about 10 minutes, then lower the heat to 180C/350F/Gas 4 and continue to roast for 1½-2 hours, depending on how well cooked you like your lamb.

**9** Transfer the joint to a warmed serving dish and keep hot. Drain off the excess fat from the roasting tin, then transfer to the top of the cooker to make the gravy. Add the stock and wine to the tin and bring to the boil, stirring to scrape off any browned pieces from the base of the tin. Allow to bubble and reduce slightly, then add the redcurrant jelly and stir until it melts. Taste and adjust seasoning, then pour into a sauceboat and keep hot.

**10** Remove the foil from the bone ends of the meat, then decorate each bone with a cutlet frill, a small cherry tomato or a baby onion parboiled and lightly browned in butter. To serve, carve the joint into cutlets, allowing 2 per person.

---

## Cook's Notes

**TIME**
30 minutes to prepare the stuffing; the apricots need to be soaked overnight. The meat takes 30 minutes to prepare, and cooking time is 1¾-2¼ hours.

**COOK'S TIP**
Most good butchers will prepare a crown roast for you if given at least 48 hours notice. Some will even make a stuffing for you as well.

**BUYING GUIDE**
If coriander seeds are not available, commercially ground coriander is a slightly milder substitute.

●510 calories/2125 kj per portion

---

### TO PREPARE A CROWN ROAST

**1** *Remove the skin on the fatty side of the joints.*

**3** *On meaty side, make slits between cutlet bases.*

**2** *Remove fat and meat from bone ends. Cut away gristle and meat in between. Scrape clean.*

**4** *Sew joints together. Fat inside, bend joint round to form a ring. Sew together.*

# IRELAND

In the best traditions of regional cooking, Irish stew was originally made from ingredients raised or grown locally on the farms. The toughest cuts of mutton or goat became tender during long, slow cooking and imparted their rich, strong flavour to potatoes and onions, the only vegetables included in an authentic Irish stew. Nowadays the stew is made with lamb, and other vegetables such as carrots, turnips or celery may be included.

# Irish stew

SERVES 4-6

**1.5 kg/3-3½ lb best end of neck lamb chops, trimmed of excess fat (see Buying guide)**
**1 kg/2 lb potatoes, cut into 5 mm/ ¼ inch slices**
**500 g/1 lb onions, sliced**
**1 tablespoon chopped fresh parsley**
**1 tablespoon chopped fresh thyme, or 1 teaspoon dried thyme**
**salt and freshly ground black pepper**
**425 ml/¾ pint water**
**1 tablespoon chopped fresh parsley, to garnish**

**1** Heat the oven to 140C/275F/Gas 1.
**2** Arrange one-third of the sliced potatoes in a layer in the base of a large casserole. Add a layer of one-third of the sliced onions, sprinkle with some of the parsley and thyme and season with salt and pepper. Arrange half the lamb chops on top and season with more salt and pepper. Make a further layer each of potatoes and onions. Sprinkle with herbs and season with salt and pepper. Arrange the remaining lamb chops on top and season with more salt and pepper. Cover the meat with the remaining onions and herbs and arrange a final layer of potatoes on top, overlapping the slices so that they cover the onions completely (see Step).
**3** Pour over the water and cover the casserole tightly with a piece of foil and then with the lid.
**4** Cook the casserole in the oven for 3 hours, checking from time to time to make sure that the liquid has not evaporated too much. If the casserole does begin to look dry, add a little boiling water to moisten it slightly.
**5** Remove the casserole from the oven and remove the foil. Run a knife around the edge of the casserole, garnish with chopped parsley and serve at once.

## LAYERING POTATOES

*Arrange the sliced potatoes overlapping to form a 'crust' on top of the final layer of sliced onions.*

---

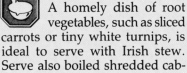

## Cook's Notes

### TIME
Preparation takes about 30 minutes, cooking in the oven 3 hours.

### BUYING GUIDE
Best end of neck chops give a very tasty sauce, much of the flavour coming from the bones which are cooked as part of the dish. Scrag end of neck, a less expensive cut of lamb, also gives good results. Ask the butcher to chop it into serving-size pieces.

### SERVING IDEAS
A homely dish of root vegetables, such as sliced carrots or tiny white turnips, is ideal to serve with Irish stew. Serve also boiled shredded cabbage tossed in butter and chunks of warm homemade Irish soda bread,
A glass of Guinness goes well with Irish stew.

### COOK'S TIP
If you do not wish to use the oven, this is an ideal dish to cook in an electric slow cooker. Follow manufacturer's instructions for timing.
The stew may also be cooked on top of the cooker in a large heavy-based saucepan. Grease the pan before layering the ingredients in it, then cook for 2½-3 hours over very low heat. If possible, stand the pan on an asbestos mat.

●925 calories/3875 kj per portion

# SCOTLAND

**Although shortbread is very popular all year round and in all parts of the country, it is particularly associated with Scotland. It is served at Christmas time and at Hogmanay when it is offered to first-footers in return for the good luck they are thought to bring.**

Shortbread is quick and easy to make, but relies for its success on long, slow baking and top-quality ingredients—butter is essential to make each piece, literally, melt in the mouth.

Traditionally, shortbread is shaped in attractive wooden moulds, the most usual being decorated with a thistle design, but it can also be shaped by hand.

## Shortbread

MAKES 2 SHORTBREADS
225 g/8 oz plain flour
good pinch of salt
100 g/4 oz rice flour or ground rice
225 g/8 oz butter
100 g/4 oz caster sugar
caster sugar, for finishing

**1** Heat the oven to 180C/350F/Gas 4. Line 2 baking trays with ungreased greaseproof paper.
**2** Sift together the flour, salt and rice flour on to a plate.
**3** Using your fingertips, rub the butter and sugar together on a pastry board or marble slab until well blended.
**4** Gradually work the flour mixture into the butter and sugar, keeping the mixing as light as possible, until all the ingredients are blended together into a large, smooth ball of dough.
**5** Divide dough in half and place on prepared baking trays. Or place each piece of dough in a 17.5 cm/7 inch shortbread mould (see Preparation). Pat each piece out with the heel of the hand to form a 16 cm/6½ inch round 1-2 cm/½-¾ inch thick (see Step 1).
**6** Neaten the edges if slightly cracked by pressing together with a knife, then crimp the edges, using a finger and thumb (see Step 2).

## Cook's Notes

**TIME**
Preparation takes about 25 minutes, baking about 40-45 minutes.

**PREPARATION**
Lightly brush the mould with a little oil, then blot off the excess with absorbent paper. Dust with a mixture of 1 teaspoon plain flour and 1 teaspoon caster sugar, then gently tap to remove any surplus. Place the dough in the mould and press in with the fingers so mould is filled evenly and shortbread pressed well down into pattern on base. Invert mould over baking tray lined with ungreased grease-proof paper. Tap edge gently against edge of tray until shortbread loosens. Carefully turn out. Prick round edges of pattern with fork. Bake as in stage 8.

**WATCHPOINT**
To make sure the mixture does not become oily, use cool hands and do not overwork at this stage.

**COOK'S TIP**
If baking trays will not fit on one shelf, swap the trays halfway through baking time to ensure even cooking.

●205 calories/850 kj per piece

## SHAPING AND FINISHING SHORTBREAD

**1** *Use the heel of the hand to shape the shortbread carefully into a round.*

**2** *Use finger and thumb to crimp the edge of the shortbread decoratively.*

**7** Prick the shortbread all over in circles with a fork so that it does not rise during cooking. Place a 17.5 cm/7 inch flan ring round each shortbread, if liked, to keep edge neat during baking.
**8** Bake in the centre of the oven for 40-45 minutes or until pale golden brown, covering if necessary with greaseproof paper towards the end of baking to avoid overbrowning the shortbread (see Cook's tip).
**9** Remove the shortbreads from the oven and immediately score each into 8 sections with a sharp knife, taking care not to cut right through. Sprinkle the top of each shortbread with sugar. Leave to cool slightly, then transfer to a wire rack until quite cold. To serve, cut right through the scored sections or break them with your fingers.

# WALES

*Bara brith* (pronounced 'breeth') means 'speckled bread' in Welsh, and is a spiced fruit loaf traditional to all Celtic countries. In Wales, country people have always been famed for their sweet breads, and Bara brith was a customary treat at Christmas, Easter and harvest time. Originally it was made with yeast, but self-raising flour is quicker and easier to use.

## Bara brith

MAKES 2 × 1 KG/2 LB LOAVES
    (see Economy)
250 g/8 oz sultanas (see Cook's tips)
125 g/4 oz currants
125 g/4 oz seedless raisins
500 g/1 lb light soft brown sugar
600 ml/1 pint warm strong tea, strained
1 egg, lightly beaten
750 g/1½ lb self-raising flour (see Cook's tips)
2 teaspoons ground mixed spice
vegetable oil, for greasing
1 tablespoon clear honey, to glaze

1 Put the sultanas, currants, raisins and sugar in a bowl. Pour in the tea and stir well. Cover with a clean tea-towel and leave overnight.
2 Heat the oven to 170C/325F/Gas 3.
3 Grease and line with greaseproof paper two 1 kg/2 lb loaf tins (see Steps). Grease the lining paper.
4 Stir the beaten egg well into the fruit and sugar mixture. Sift together the flour and spice, then stir into the mixture until thoroughly combined.
5 Divide the mixture equally between the prepared tins. Smooth the surface of each.
6 Bake the loaves in the oven for 1½ hours, then lower the heat to 140C/275F/Gas 1 and bake for a further 1½ hours, until a warmed fine skewer inserted into the loaves comes out clean.
7 Leave the loaves for a few minutes until cool enough to handle, then turn them out on to a wire rack. Invert the loaves the right way up.
8 Put the honey in a small saucepan and heat very gently. Brush the tops of the warm loaves, to glaze. Leave until completely cold.

## Cook's Notes

**TIME**
Allow overnight soaking time. Preparation then takes about 15 minutes. Baking takes 3 hours and glazing 5 minutes.

**ECONOMY**
As Bara brith stores and freezes well, it is well worth baking 2 loaves, to save on fuel. If you prefer to make just 1 loaf, you can of course simply halve the quantities given in the recipe.

**COOK'S TIPS**
Just 1 or 2 types of dried fruit may be used, providing the total weight is 500 g/1 lb.
If you prefer, use plain flour sifted with 2 tablespoons baking powder.
The bread may be eaten as soon as it is completely cold, but the flavour and texture improve if it is stored in an airtight tin for 1 week.

**SERVING IDEAS**
Serve cut into slices and spread with butter. Honey or jam go well with Bara brith for tea, or try it with a wedge of Caerphilly or Cheddar cheese for a snack lunch.

**FREEZING**
Open freeze the baked glazed loaves until the glaze is firm, then wrap in foil, seal, label and freeze for up to 6 months. To serve: unwrap and defrost at room temperature for 4-6 hours.

● 3030 calories/12725 kj per loaf

### TO LINE A LOAF TIN

1 *Use base of tin to mark grease-proof paper with pencil. Cut out rectangle along line.*

2 *Cut greaseproof strip 5 cm/2 inches wider than tin depth and long enough to go round tin.*

3 *Fold in 1 cm/½ inch border along 1 long side of strip. Snip as far as fold.*

4 *Fit strip inside greased tin with snipped border on base. Place greaseproof rectangle on top.*

# FINLAND

In Finland, the traditional food for a family feast is a casserole of mixed meats accompanied by rice-filled pasties. Both these dishes come from Karelia, a region that was once in eastern Finland but is now part of the Soviet Union. On farms, the hotpot was put into a hot brick oven early in the morning and left to simmer all day until the dish was cooked and the oven nearly cold. Tasty and warming, these dishes are ideal food for cold days.

## Karelian hotpot

**SERVES 6-8**

500 g/1 lb chuck steak, cut into 2.5 cm/1 inch cubes
500 g/1 lb boned shoulder of lamb, cut into 2.5 cm/1 inch cubes
500 g/1 lb boned shoulder or loin of pork, cut into 2.5 cm/1 inch cubes
350 g/12 oz lamb kidneys, halved, cores removed
3 large onions, thickly sliced
1 teaspoon salt
2 teaspoons ground allspice
600 ml/1 pint hot beef stock

1 Heat the oven to 200C/400F/Gas 6.
2 Put all the cubed meat and the kidneys into a large ovenproof casserole and mix well. Top with the sliced onions.
3 Add the salt and allspice to the hot stock. Stir well to mix and pour into the casserole.
4 Cover tightly and cook in the oven for about 30 minutes or until the stock is bubbling. Turn the oven down to 170C/325F/Gas 3 and cook for a further 3½-4 hours until the meats are very tender. Stir well, taste and adjust seasoning (the dish should be quite salty). Serve hot with the pasties.

### Cook's Notes

**TIME**
Preparation 20 minutes, cooking 4-4½ hours.

**SERVING IDEAS**
Serve with a beetroot and apple salad.

●695 calories/2925 kj per portion

### Cook's Notes

**TIME**
Total preparation time is about 1 hour, cooking time 15 minutes. Allow at least 30 minutes for chilling the pastry and cooling the filling.

**COOK'S TIPS**
The pastry may be made the day before and chilled overnight in cling film.

**VARIATION**
Use 175-250 g/6-9 oz mashed potato in place of the rice filling.

**BUYING GUIDE**
Rye flour, available from health food shops is vital in this recipe.

●165 calories/700 kj per pasty

## Karelian pasties

**MAKES 12-14 PASTIES**
150 g/5 oz rye flour (see Buying guide)
150 g/5 oz plain flour
½ teaspoon salt
150 ml/¼ pint cold water

**FILLING**
150 ml/¼ pint water
50 g/2 oz pudding rice
300 ml/½ pint milk
¼ teaspoon salt

**GLAZE**
2 tablespoons water
25 g/1 oz butter

**TO SERVE**
50 g/2 oz butter, softened
2 hard-boiled eggs, mashed

1 First make the filling: bring the water to the boil over high heat. Add the rice, milk and salt and bring back to the boil, stirring. Lower the heat, cover the pan and simmer very gently, stirring occasionally, for about 45 minutes or until all the liquid is absorbed and the mixture is thick and creamy. Set aside to cool.
2 To make the pastry: sift the rye and plain flours into a large bowl with the salt. Add the water, and quickly mix with one hand to form a stiff dough.
3 Knead the dough for 1-2 minutes until it leaves your hand cleanly as you work it. Add more flour or water if necessary. Wrap in cling film and refrigerate for at least 30 minutes.
4 Heat the oven to 240C/475F/Gas 9. Dust a large baking sheet with rye flour.
5 Roll the pastry on a floured board and cut, shape and fill the pasties (see Steps). Transfer to the prepared baking sheet.
6 Bake in the oven for 10-15 minutes until the undersides of the pasties are light brown and the rice filling is set and light golden on top.
7 Meanwhile, make the glaze: boil the water and add the butter. Heat until the butter has melted.
8 As soon as the pasties are cooked, dip them in the butter and water mixture and turn them until coated all over to soften the pastry.
9 To serve: mix the softened butter with the mashed hard-boiled eggs and spoon on top of the warm pasties. Serve at once.

## TO SHAPE PASTIES

**1** On a board floured with rye flour, roll the pastry into a long sausage about 4.5 cm/3⁄4 inches in diameter. Cut into 2 cm/3⁄4 inch lengths.

**2** Roll each piece into a thin oval about 15 × 10 cm/ 6 × 4 inches. Spread 1 tablespoon filling over the centre.

**3** Fold in and flute the pastry edges, leaving a little filling showing in the centre.

# NORWAY

Fish in many forms – fresh, smoked, salted and pickled – is a staple of the Norwegian diet. There are hundreds of Norwegian fish recipes, but poached fish balls or *fiskebollar* is one of the most popular. For everyday meals they are served plain, but for special occasions they are served with a prawn sauce, either as an hors d'oeuvre or main course accompanied by mashed potatoes and another root vegetable such as glazed swedes.

## Fiskebollar

SERVES 4
**750 g/1½ lb haddock fillets, skinned (see Buying guide)**
**sea salt (see Did you know)**
**freshly ground black pepper**
**¼ teaspoon ground mace**
**large pinch of freshly grated nutmeg**
**3 tablespoons cornflour**
**4 tablespoons double cream**
**700 ml/1¼ pints milk (see Variations)**

SAUCE
**25 g/1 oz butter**
**25 g/1 oz plain flour**
**175 g/6 oz cooked peeled prawns, defrosted if frozen**

GARNISH
**dill sprigs**
**few unpeeled prawns (optional)**

1 Mince the fish by passing it twice through the fine blades of a mincer or by working it in a food processor.
2 Transfer the minced fish to a large bowl. Add 1 teaspoon sea salt, a generous grinding of black pepper, the mace, nutmeg, cornflour and cream. Beat with a fork for 5-10 minutes until the fish mixture is very smooth.
3 Divide the mixture into 20 portions. Roll each one between the hands into an evenly shaped ball.
4 Heat the oven to 110C/225F/Gas ¼.
5 Pour the milk into a large wide saucepan. Season with salt and pepper and bring just to the boil. Lower the heat and, using a slotted spoon, carefully put the fish balls into the pan. Simmer, uncovered, for 10-15 minutes or until the fish

balls are firm and cooked through.
6 Remove pan from the heat. Remove the fish balls with a slotted spoon and arrange them on a warmed large serving platter. Keep them warm in the oven while making the sauce.
7 Measure 300 ml/½ pint of the cooking liquid into a jug. Melt the butter in a small saucepan. Sprinkle in the flour and stir over low heat for 1-2 minutes until straw-coloured. Remove from the heat and gradually stir in the cooking liquid. Return to the heat and simmer, stirring, until thick and smooth. Add the peeled prawns, taste and adjust seasoning, then simmer for 1-2 minutes, stirring, until the prawns are heated through.
8 Spoon the sauce over the fish balls. Garnish with dill and unpeeled prawns, if liked, and serve at once, while piping hot.

## Glazed swedes

SERVES 4
**500 g/1 lb swedes, cut into 4 cm/1½ inch cubes**
**25 g/1 oz butter**
**1 tablespoon dark syrup (see Buying guide)**
**salt and freshly ground black pepper**

1 Heat the butter in a flameproof casserole, add the swedes and fry quickly over brisk heat, turning, to brown. Add the syrup and turn to coat the swedes.
2 Season with salt, lower heat and cook very gently, turning occasionally, for about 30 minutes. Season with pepper and transfer to a warmed serving dish. Serve at once, with the fiskebollar.

## Cook's Notes

**Fiskebollar**

**TIME**
Preparation takes about 30 minutes. Cooking time is only about 25 minutes.

**BUYING GUIDE**
Flake, dogfish, huss and rigg are alternative names which cover a variety of small sharks. Flake has firm, meaty flesh.
  The skin of fish fillets weighs much more than might be expected, so if buying the fish unskinned, allow an extra 125 g/4 oz for the weight of the skin.

**VARIATIONS**
Fish stock may be substituted for half the quantity of milk, if liked.
  The fish mixture can be shaped into 40 smaller balls and served as a starter for 8 people.

●450 calories/1900 kj per portion

**Glazed swedes**

**TIME**
Preparation takes about 5 minutes, cooking time is about 35 minutes.

**BUYING GUIDE**
Dark syrup, less refined, darker in colour and stronger tasting than golden syrup, is available from large supermarkets: if unobtainable, use half golden syrup, half black treacle.

●80 calories/350 kj per portion

# DENMARK

*Frikadeller*, the egg-shaped Danish version of meat balls, are one of Denmark's most popular dishes. The Danes like to eat a light lunch of their famous open sandwiches (*smørrebrød*) and then have a hot, early evening meal. This is when Frikadeller are usually served, and most Danish families eat them at least once a week.

## Frikadeller

**SERVES 4**

500 g/1 lb finely minced pork (see Buying guide)

2 tablespoons plain flour

150 ml/¼ pint milk

1 egg, beaten

1 small onion, grated or minced

½ teaspoon ground allspice (optional)

½ teaspoon salt

½ teaspoon freshly ground black pepper

100 g/4 oz unsalted butter, melted (see Buying guide)

1 Heat oven to 130C/250F/Gas ½.

2 Put the minced pork in a large bowl, sprinkle in the flour and very gradually stir in the milk to mix thoroughly (see Cook's tip). Stir in the egg, onion and allspice, if using, and season with salt and pepper.

3 Heat half the melted butter in a frying-pan. Dip a tablespoon in the remaining butter and then scoop up a heaped spoonful of the pork mixture (see Step).

4 Shape and fry frikadeller over moderate heat for 5 minutes on each side, adding more butter as needed and dipping the spoon in the butter each time. Transfer to a warmed serving dish and keep hot while you fry the remainder. Serve hot (see Serving ideas).

### SHAPING FRIKADELLER

*Scoop up a heaped tablespoon of minced pork mixture, then pat to a neat round against inside of bowl.*

### TIME
Preparation takes about 15 minutes but allow 2-3 days for marinating. Making the sauce takes about 10 minutes, but it should stand for about 1 hour before serving to let the flavours blend.

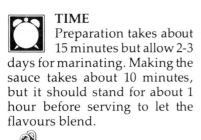

### BUYING GUIDE
When buying the salmon, ask the fishmonger to fillet it for you. If fresh salmon is not available, use frozen and defrost it first.

Swedish mustard, which is mild and sweet, is best for this sauce, but American mustard, which is also mild and more readily available, is a very good substitute.

### DID YOU KNOW
It is believed that the name *gravlax* (*grav* means grave) suggests that the salmon used to be 'buried' in a dark, cool cellar to marinate.

### SERVING IDEAS
Serve the salmon as a starter with hot white toast, or thinly sliced brown bread and butter, and lemon wedges. Or serve for a light lunch with bread and a salad.

### ECONOMY
Ask your fishmonger for the tail piece, which is sometimes cheaper.

● 240 calories/1000 kj per portion

---

**MARINATING THE SALMON**

Put the second fillet over the first so that the thick end of the top piece lies over the thin end of the bottom piece.

**TWO METHODS OF CUTTING THE SALMON**

**1** *Start a few inches from the tail end and cut long, thin slices with a long, sharp knife, keeping the blade almost horizontally against the salmon.*

**2** *Using a long sharp knife, cut the salmon into vertical slices about 5 mm/¼ inch thick across the entire width of the salmon.*

# SWEDEN

Not so long ago, salmon was such common fare in Sweden, that in some parts of the country contracts of employment stated that employees did not have to eat it more than three times a week! Today, however, when salmon is no longer abundant in Swedish rivers, it is considered a great delicacy, and reserved only for special occasions.

Ideally, *gravlax* (see Did you know) should be made with fresh dill which has a superb flavour. Fresh dill, however, is not readily available (despite the fact that it is very easy to grow from seed in a pot). For this reason our recipe uses the dried variety, called dillweed, which is a good substitute provided it is still aromatic.

## Gravlax

SERVES 8

**fresh salmon (filleted weight 750 g/1½ lb, see Buying guide)**
3½ teaspoons salt
4 teaspoons sugar
1 teaspoon white peppercorns, coarsely crushed
2 tablespoons dillweed
lemon twists, to garnish

SAUCE
3 tablespoons dillweed
3 tablespoons hot water
6 tablespoons mild mustard
   (see Buying guide)
2 tablespoons sugar
1 tablespoon red wine vinegar
2 tablespoons vegetable oil
salt and freshly ground black pepper

1 Wipe the salmon fillets with absorbent paper and remove any bones.
2 Mix the salt, sugar and peppercorns together and put about one-third in the bottom of a shallow dish. Lay one salmon fillet in the dish, skin side down, and sprinkle with half the remaining mixture and the dillweed. Put the second salmon fillet over the first one, skin side up. Lay its thick end on top of the thin end of the bottom fillet so that the fillets are flat (see Steps). Rub the remaining mixture into the skin.
3 Cover the salmon with foil. Put a dish on top of the fish and put weights or heavy tins on it to press the salmon pieces together. Refrigerate for 2-3 days, turning the pieces occasionally.
4 To make the sauce: put the dillweed in a small bowl and pour over the hot water. Leave for 5 minutes.
5 Meanwhile, mix the mustard, sugar and vinegar in a bowl, stir until the sugar has dissolved completely, then gradually add the oil and whisk to a smooth sauce.
6 Drain the dillweed thoroughly, add to the sauce and season with salt and pepper to taste. Leave in a cool place for 1 hour before serving.
7 To serve: remove dillweed from the fish and scrape off peppercorns with a knife. Cut the fish like smoked salmon, into thin slices, or straight across into chunkier pieces (see Steps). Discard the skin. Arrange the slices on a serving plate and garnish with lemon twists. Pour the sauce into a sauceboat and serve separately.

# Cook's Notes

### TIME
Preparation takes about 30 minutes, using ready-minced pork. Cooking takes about 40 minutes.

### COOK'S TIP
The mixture should be slightly slack—not as stiff as some meat ball or rissole mixtures.

### VARIATIONS
Breadcrumbs or crushed rusks instead of flour, and plain or soda water instead of milk are sometimes used to mix frikadeller.

In Denmark, frikadeller are most often made with pork, but a mixture of pork and beef or pork and veal can also be used.

Frikadeller can be made from cold left-over meat with a little minced smoked bacon added. This type is known in Denmark by the rather sombre name of *døde* (dead) frikadeller.

### SERVING IDEAS
In Denmark, frikadeller are usually served hot with boiled potatoes and gravy made from the pan juices. For special occasions, it is customary to serve them with sugar-browned potatoes (small potatoes browned in a caramel mixture of butter and sugar) as well as plain boiled potatoes and a second vegetable such as creamed spinach or curly kale.

Frikadeller can also be served warm with potato salad and a green salad. In Denmark, they are used cold in open sandwiches and these are a great favourite with school children in their lunch boxes.

### BUYING GUIDE
Some butchers and supermarkets sell ready-minced pork, but if it is not available ask for blade, spare-rib or hand. Your butcher will mince it for you, if you wish, or you can do it yourself at home. It must be really finely minced, to achieve a close, but light and springy texture.

Danish dairy products are world-famous, and their unsalted butter is renowned for its flavour.

●580 calories/2430 kj per portion

# BELGIUM

*Waterzootje*, Flemish for fisherman's soup, was originally a staple dish in the small fishing communities along the Belgian coast. Over the centuries it has become more of a chunky fish stew than a soup, and there is also a version using chicken. Cooked with white wine and cream, *Waterzootje* may be made from any kind of sea or freshwater fish.

## Waterzootje

**SERVES 8**

2 kg/4-4½ lb white fish, cleaned, filleted and skinned, trimmings reserved (see Buying guide)
3 onions, sliced
3 cloves garlic (optional)
425 ml/¾ pint medium white wine
juice of 1 lemon
sprig of thyme
2 sage leaves, or pinch of dried sage
2 bay leaves
6 parsley sprigs
salt and freshly ground black pepper
50 g/2 oz butter
500 g/1 lb leeks, chopped
1 small head celery, chopped
4 tablespoons chopped fresh parsley

**TO SERVE**

2 egg yolks, beaten
4 tablespoons single cream
2 tablespoons snipped chives
4 extra tablespoons single cream (optional)

1 Put the fish heads, tails, bones and trimmings in a very large saucepan with the onions, garlic, if using, wine, lemon juice, thyme, sage, bay leaves, parsley sprigs and salt and pepper.
2 Pour in 1.75 L/3 pints fresh cold water to cover. Bring to the boil, then lower the heat, cover and simmer gently for 30 minutes.
3 Meanwhile, melt the butter in a large saucepan, add the leeks, celery and chopped parsley and cook gently, stirring from time to time, for about 5 minutes. Season with salt and pepper. Pour in 1.75L/3 pints fresh cold water to cover. Bring to the boil, then lower the heat, cover and simmer very gently

for about 30 minutes, until the vegetables are tender but firm.
4 Meanwhile, pat the fish fillets dry with absorbent paper. Using a very sharp knife, cut them into 2.5-4 cm/1-1½ inch pieces.
5 Strain and measure the fish stock and, if necessary, boil rapidly to reduce to 1.5 L/2½ pints. Strain the vegetables and measure 1.5 L/2½ pints of the stock. Pour both stocks into a very large saucepan or fish kettle (see Cook's tip) and add the cooked vegetables. Taste and adjust the seasoning.
6 Bring the contents of the pan to the boil, then lower the heat to the

very lowest simmering point. [!] Gently lower the fish pieces into the pan, cover and simmer for no longer than 5 minutes, until the fish is just cooked. [!] Remove at once from the heat.
7 In a warmed soup tureen or large bowl, combine the egg yolks with 4 tablespoons cream and the chives.
8 Thoroughly blend 1 ladle of hot soup with the egg yolk mixture then very carefully pour in the rest of the soup, making sure that the fish pieces do not break up. Serve at once in warmed soup bowls, with a spoonful of cream swirled on the top of each, if liked.

## Cook's Notes

### TIME
Preparation takes about 25 minutes. Cooking the fish and vegetable stock takes about 30 minutes, finishing the soup, including cooking the fish, takes about 15 minutes.

### BUYING GUIDE
Try to buy the fish from a wet fishmonger and experiment with some of the more exotic types, combining the more expensive kinds with those that are less costly. Bream, snapper, cod and plaice, or bass, John Dory, haddock and whiting are good combinations. If you use frozen fish fillets or steaks, you will still need spare fish trimmings from a fishmonger for the stock.

### VARIATION
If liked, 250 g/9 oz sliced carrots may be cooked with the leeks and celery, to make the dish more substantial and colourful.

### SERVING IDEAS
Serve the soup as a main course with hot French bread and unsalted butter, and accompany it with a dish of plain boiled potatoes, to make a complete and filling meal.

### COOK'S TIP
A fish kettle—a large, narrow pan with a tray or grid on which the fish is placed and then poached—is invaluable as the fish can be removed easily without any danger of disintegrating.

### WATCHPOINTS
The stock must be at the very lowest simmering point—there should be barely a tremor on the surface—so that when the fish pieces are added they do not overcook or the soup will be ruined.
Watch the fish carefully once it is immersed, as it cooks extremely quickly.

●355 calories/1500 kj per portion

# GERMANY

*Sauerbraten* (sour-sweet beef) is the German pot-roasted equivalent of a Sunday roast beef joint. Cooked in a very tasty spiced sauce, *Sauerbraten* is traditionally served with potato dumplings or buttered noodles and a dish of stewed apple.

## Sauerbraten

**SERVES 4**

1 kg/2 lb topside of beef, rolled and tied
50 g/2 oz lard
3 tablespoons plain flour
25 g/1 oz butter
1 tablespoon light soft brown sugar
2 tablespoons seedless raisins (optional)

MARINADE
425 ml/¾ pint red wine
300 ml/½ pint water
150 ml/¼ pint wine vinegar
1 large onion, thinly sliced
1 large carrot, thinly sliced
1 celery stalk, chopped
1 bay leaf
6 black whole peppercorns, crushed
3 allspice berries
3 cloves
1 teaspoon salt

1 Place the beef in a bowl large enough to contain it and also the marinade.
2 To make the marinade: put all the ingredients in a saucepan and bring slowly to the boil. Pour over the beef and allow to cool. Cover the bowl with cling film and refrigerate for 3 days, turning the beef each day in the marinade.
3 Remove the beef from the marinade and pat dry with absorbent paper. Put the marinade in a saucepan and gently heat through.
4 Meanwhile, melt the lard in a deep flameproof casserole, add the beef and fry over moderate heat, turning to seal on all sides (see Cook's tips). Sprinkle the beef with 2 tablespoons of the flour and continue turning until it is completely browned all over.
5 Pour over half the marinade, lower the heat, cover and simmer for 1 hour. Pour over the remaining marinade and continue to cook for a further 30-60 minutes, or until the beef is tender and cooked through (the juices run clear when the meat is pierced with a skewer).
6 Pour off the marinade into a bowl and leave to cool. Cover the casserole and keep warm in the oven turned to lowest setting. Skim the fat from the surface of the cooled marinade, and then strain it (see Cook's tips).
7 Melt the butter in a small saucepan, sprinkle in the remaining flour and the sugar and stir over low heat for 1-2 minutes. Remove from heat and gradually stir in the skimmed marinade. Return to the heat and simmer, stirring, until thick and smooth. Remove from the heat. Stir in the raisins, if using. Return the sauce to the heat and reheat gently, stirring all the time.
8 Carve the beef into slices, then arrange overlapping on a warmed serving dish. Spoon over a little of the sauce. Serve with potato and bacon dumplings (see recipe) or buttered noodles and the remaining sauce, handed round separately in a warmed bowl.

## Cook's Notes

**Sauerbraten**

 **TIME**
Preparing the *Sauerbraten* takes about 10 minutes. Allow 3 days marinating time. Cooking the dish takes about 2 hours.

**COOK'S TIPS**
Use kitchen tongs to hold the beef joint securely as you turn it in the casserole, so that the fat does not spit dangerously.
Reserve the beef fat skimmed from the marinade stock and store in the refrigerator for use as a delicious savoury spread for toast.

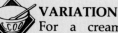 **VARIATION**
For a creamy sauce, omit the raisins and stir 150 ml/¼ pint soured cream into the sauce at the end of stage 7. Reheat very gently but on no account allow the sauce to boil.

 **FREEZING**
Freeze the sliced cooked beef in the sauce in a rigid container for up to 6 months. To serve: defrost at room temperature for 3 hours, transfer to a saucepan and reheat gently, adding 1-2 tablespoons water to prevent the sauce from sticking. Stir gently when the meat slices can be separated. Heat through but do not allow to boil.

 **SERVING IDEAS**
Serve a light beer to drink with *Sauerbraten*, as the Germans do.
Serve a bowl of stewed apple spiced with cloves separately.

●585 calories/2450 kj per portion

**Dumplings**

 **TIME**
Preparation, including boiling the potatoes, takes about 35 minutes. Cooking the dumplings takes about 15 minutes.

**WATCHPOINT**
It is essential to keep the water boiling all the time, otherwise the dumplings may break up.

●100 calories/425 kj each

# Potato and bacon dumplings

**MAKES 8**
500 g/1 lb potatoes
salt
[!] 75 g/3 oz back bacon rashers, rinds removed, finely chopped
1 egg, beaten
50 g/2 oz fresh white breadcrumbs
2 teaspoons cornflour
¼ teaspoon freshly grated nutmeg
vegetable oil, for greasing

1 Put the potatoes in a large saucepan of salted water. Bring to the boil and boil gently for 15-20 minutes.
2 Meanwhile, brush the base of a large heavy-based frying-pan with oil. Put the chopped bacon in the pan and fry over moderate heat, stirring several times, for 3 minutes.
3 Bring a large saucepan of lightly salted water to the boil.
4 Drain the potatoes well and mash until smooth. Stir in egg, breadcrumbs, cornflour, ½ teaspoon salt, nutmeg and bacon. Mix then shape into dumplings (see Step).
5 Lower the dumplings into the boiling salted water and boil gently for 15 minutes. [!]
6 Using a slotted spoon, transfer the dumplings to a warmed serving dish and serve hot with the beef.

## TO SHAPE DUMPLINGS

*Cut round of dumpling mixture into 8 equal wedges. Shape each wedge into a ball, with well-floured hands.*

The Black Forest region of south-west Germany is a famous cherry-growing area, and chocolate and cherry cakes have been popular there for over a hundred years. Black Forest torte, with its rich cream and cherry filling and kirsch flavour is probably the most famous chocolate cake in the world. It makes an elegant and sophisticated dessert for any special occasion.

# Black Forest torte

MAKES 8-10 SLICES

150 g/5 oz plain flour
2 teaspoons bicarbonate of soda
1 teaspoon coffee powder
1 tablespoon cocoa powder
6 eggs, separated
150 g/5 oz caster sugar
1 teaspoon lemon juice
75 g/3 oz plain dessert chocolate, finely grated
pinch of salt
melted butter, for greasing
1 tablespoon each plain flour and caster sugar, for dusting

FILLING
1 kg/2 lb Morello cherries (see Buying guide), stoned
100 g/4 oz granulated sugar
600 ml/1 pint water
150 ml/¼ pint kirsch
425 ml/¾ pint double cream
3 tablespoons caster sugar
25 g/1 oz chocolate, coarsely grated or flaked, for decoration

1 First prepare the cherries for the filling: put the granulated sugar in a large, heavy-based saucepan with the water. Heat gently until the sugar has dissolved, then bring to the boil and boil rapidly for 2 minutes without stirring. Remove from the heat and carefully add the cherries, then return to the heat and poach gently for 10 minutes.

2 Remove the cherries from the syrup with a slotted spoon and set aside to cool. Boil the syrup rapidly for 2 minutes until thickened. Remove from the heat, measure out 75 ml/3 fl oz and leave to cool.

3 Heat the oven to 180C/350F/Gas 4. Grease the base and sides of two 23 cm/9 inch loose-bottomed cake tins

with melted butter. Line the base of each tin with a circle of greaseproof paper and grease the paper. Mix together the tablespoons of flour and sugar, sprinkle over the insides of the tins, then shake the tins until evenly coated. Shake off any excess.

4 To make the cakes: sift the flour 2 or 3 times with the bicarbonate of soda, coffee and cocoa powders.

5 In a bowl, set over a pan half full of simmering water, whisk egg yolks and sugar until thick enough to hold trail of whisk for 3 seconds when beaters are lifted. Mix in lemon juice and chocolate.

6 Put the egg whites and salt in a separate spotlessly clean and dry bowl. Beat together into soft peaks. Then stir 2 tablespoons of the whisked egg white into the egg yolk mixture. Using a large metal spoon, carefully fold a quarter of the remaining egg white into the mixture. Sift over 2 tablespoons of the flour mixture and carefully fold in. Repeat until all the egg white and the flour mixture have been added.

7 Divide mixture equally between the tins and lightly smooth surface to break any large air bubbles.

8 Bake in the centre of the oven, or just below for 25 minutes until the cakes are golden brown and the tops spring back when gently pressed. [!]

If you cannot get both tins on the same shelf, put one under the other and change them over halfway through the cooking time.

9 Stand the tins on a wire rack for 10 minutes. Turn cakes out, remove paper, leave to cool completely.

10 Pat the cherries dry with absorbent paper and reserve 8 for decoration. Add 125 ml/4 fl oz of the kirsch to the reserved cherry syrup.

11 Whisk the double cream into soft peaks and beat in the caster sugar. Fold in the remaining kirsch. Set aside 3-4 tablespoonfuls of cream for decoration, if wished.

12 To assemble the cake: split each sponge in 2 horizontally. Sprinkle one-third of the syrup over one bottom layer, cover with about a quarter of the cream and press half the fruit into the cream. Cover with a second sponge, sprinkle with more syrup, a layer of cream and the rest of the cherries. Lay the third sponge on top, sprinkle with the last of the syrup and cover with more whipped cream. Top with the last sponge layer and spread the remaining cream over the top and sides. Scatter grated chocolate over top and pipe rosettes of cream round the edge. Stud every other one with a cherry. Chill for 1 hour before serving.

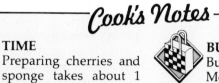

## Cook's Notes

TIME
Preparing cherries and sponge takes about 1 hour. Cooking takes 25 minutes. Allow 30 minutes for cooling, 30 minutes for assembly and a further 1 hour for chilling.

WATCHPOINT
Open the oven very gently or the cakes will collapse in the draught.

BUYING GUIDE
Buy black, sour or Morello cherries as the bright red cherries do not have enough flavour for this recipe.

VARIATIONS
An 850 g/1 lb 12 oz can of Morello or black cherries may be used.

● 670 calories/2800 kj per portion

*Lebkuchen* – spicy biscuits – are just one of the famous range of German Christmas biscuits, known collectively as *Weinachtsbäckerei* (literally, 'Christmas baking'). *Lebkuchen* are traditionally eaten on St Nicolas Day (December 6) but improve in flavour and texture if stored in an airtight container, and may be served until Twelfth Night (January 6).

# Lebkuchen

**MAKES ABOUT 60 BISCUITS**
425 g/15 oz ground almonds

50 g/2 oz candied peel, very finely chopped (see Buying guide)
2 teaspoons ground cinnamon
2 teaspoons ground cloves
2 teaspoons ground cardamom
6 eggs, separated
425 g/15 oz caster sugar

**GLAZE**
finely grated zest of 1 lemon
175 g/6 oz icing sugar, sifted
50 ml/2 fl oz boiling water
red food colouring

**TO DECORATE**
hundreds and thousands
chocolate vermicelli

1 Heat the oven to 170C/325F/Gas 3.
2 Line two 33 × 30 cm/13 × 12 inch baking trays with rice paper or non-stick baking parchment (see Cook's tips).
3 Mix the ground almonds, candied peel and spices together in a bowl and set aside.
4 Put the egg yolks and sugar into a separate large mixing bowl. Using a hand-held electric whisk, beat for about 10 minutes until the mixture is thick and cream-coloured. Or use a rotary whisk and whisk the mixture for about 20 minutes or until mixture is thick.
5 In a separate clean, dry bowl, whisk the egg whites until standing in stiff peaks. Take a large spoonful of the whisked egg whites and fold it into the yolk mixture, to loosen. Very gently fold in the remaining whisked egg whites.
6 Very gently fold the ground almond mixture into the egg and sugar mixture.
7 Place about 15 teaspoons of the mixture on each baking tray, arranging the heaps as neatly as possible and spacing them out evenly, as the mixture will spread during baking.
8 Bake the biscuits in the oven for about 15 minutes. They are ready when they are light brown and slightly soft to the touch. [!] Move the bottom tray to the higher oven shelf when removing the top tray and bake for a few minutes longer.
9 Leave the baked biscuits to cool for a few minutes on the trays, then transfer, with the lining paper, to a wire rack and leave to cool completely.
10 Repeat with the remaining mixture.
11 When the biscuits are completely cold, break off the excess rice paper with your fingers; or peel off the non-stick baking paper. Then make the glaze: mix the grated lemon zest with the icing sugar in a bowl. Very slowly add the boiling water, mix well with a fork. The glaze should be fairly runny.
12 Using a pastry brush, brush half the biscuits with the glaze. Decorate with a few hundreds and thousands as you finish each biscuit.
13 When half the biscuits have been covered with the white glaze, add 1-2 drops red colouring to the remaining glaze in the bowl, to colour it pink. Use this to glaze the remaining biscuits. Decorate with chocolate vermicelli as you finish each biscuit.
14 Leave the biscuits until the glaze has set completely, then store in an airtight tin until required.

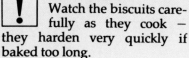

## Cook's Notes

 **TIME**
Preparation and baking take about 1 hour, decorating about 30 minutes.

**BUYING GUIDE**
Try to buy real candied peel, available from specialist food shops.

**COOK'S TIPS**
Rice paper, which can of course be eaten, is traditionally used for baking these biscuits. The excess paper is broken off the biscuits when they have cooled. In Germany where Lebkuchen are manufactured on a large commercial scale, they are often baked in special moulds, but taste as good baked on trays.

For correct consistency, do not skimp on beating time in stage 4.

**WATCHPOINT**
Watch the biscuits carefully as they cook — they harden very quickly if baked too long.

**SPECIAL OCCASION**
It is well worth making a large quantity of Lebkuchen – not only because they disappear so rapidly, but they also make attractive and unusual Christmas presents. Line a small flat basket with pink tissue paper and arrange the biscuits in it. Cover with a piece of cling film and decorate the basket with a pink satin ribbon bow.

●55 calories/235 kj per biscuit

# AUSTRIA

Crumbed veal escalopes or *schnitzels*, fried until crisp and golden, are a famous speciality of Viennese (*Wiener*) cuisine. When cooked correctly they are not at all greasy: it used to be said that the test of a perfect *schnitzel* was that it should be dry enough to allow a lady dressed in silk to sit on it without marking her skirt!

## Wiener schnitzel

SERVES 4
4 veal escalopes, each weighing
   about 175 g/6 oz
2 tablespoons plain flour
salt and freshly ground black pepper
1 egg
1 tablespoon milk
75 g/3 oz fine dry white
   breadcrumbs (see Cook's tips)
50 g/2 oz butter
4 teaspoons vegetable oil
1 large lemon, cut in wedges

1 Heat the oven to 110C/225F/Gas ¼.
2 Place the veal escalopes between 2 sheets of greaseproof paper and beat out until twice their original size (see Steps).
3 Spread the flour out on a flat plate and season well with salt and pepper. Dip the escalopes in the seasoned flour to coat them thoroughly.
4 Beat together the egg and milk in a shallow dish. Spread the breadcrumbs out on a large, flat plate. Dip the floured escalopes in the egg mixture, then in the breadcrumbs to coat evenly all over.
5 Heat half the butter and half the oil in a large frying-pan over moderately high heat. Add 2 escalopes and fry briskly for 3 minutes on each side, until golden-brown and crisp. Drain on both sides on absorbent paper, then transfer to a warmed serving dish and keep warm in the oven while cooking the other 2 escalopes.
6 Heat the remaining butter and oil, fry the remaining escalopes in the same way and drain on both sides on absorbent paper. Transfer to the serving dish, garnish with lemon wedges and serve at once.

## PREPARING THE ESCALOPES

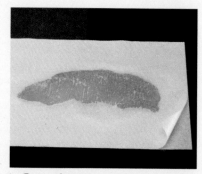

1 *On a board or work surface, place the escalope between 2 sheets of greaseproof paper, allowing plenty of room for spreading.*

2 *Beat with a rolling pin from centre to each side, until the escalope has been flattened out smoothly and evenly to about twice its original size.*

## Cook's Notes

**TIME**
Preparation takes about 20 minutes, cooking about 15 minutes.

**COOK'S TIPS**
It is best to make your own breadcrumbs for this dish: stale left-over bread and crusts are ideal and, as a guide, 1 thick slice of bread makes about 25 g/1 oz breadcrumbs. Put the bread slices in the oven at the lowest possible setting and leave for several hours to dry out and harden. Then place in a polythene bag and crush with a rolling pin until fine. It is a good idea to make more crumbs than you need for this recipe. Store in a screwtop jar and use for rissoles, fish cakes and stuffings.
If you are short of time, use golden crumbs, available in packets and drums from supermarkets.

**SERVING IDEAS**
Serve *Wiener schnitzels* with sauté potatoes and creamed spinach seasoned with freshly grated nutmeg.
In Vienna, a very light white wine such as Grinzinger (from the village of Grinzing outside Vienna) would accompany the schnitzels: this wine is always drunk in the year of its vintage (the year it is made, which is why it is referred to as a very 'young' wine), and served chilled in earthenware pitchers. Grinzinger is not exported, so you can serve any well-chilled dry or medium white wine: an Austrian Schluck would make a good substitute or a German Liebfraumilch.
For Holstein schnitzel – top each cooked escalope with a fried egg and garnish with anchovies and a few capers.

●405 calories/1700 kj per portion

**The Austrians are famous for their rich *torten* or cakes, and one of the best-known is Sachertorte: a moist, chocolate sponge cake glazed with jam, then covered with a thick, shiny chocolate icing. It was created by Franz Sacher, a master pastry-cook and founder of Vienna's famous Hotel Sacher.**

# Sachertorte

MAKES 12 SLICES

175 g/6 oz plain dessert chocolate, broken into small pieces (see Buying guide)
2 tablespoons water
175 g/6 oz butter, softened
175 g/6 oz icing sugar, sifted
6 large eggs, separated
2-3 drops vanilla essence
150 g/5 oz plain flour, sifted
8 tablespoons apricot jam
melted butter, for greasing

ICING
150 g/5 oz plain dessert chocolate, broken into small pieces
5 tablespoons water
100 g/4 oz icing sugar, sifted
2½ teaspoons glycerine (see Buying guide)

1 Heat the oven to 180C/350F/Gas 4. Prepare a loose-based deep 23 cm/9 inch round cake tin (see Steps).
2 To make the cake: put the chocolate and water in a small heatproof bowl; place over a saucepan of gently simmering water and leave, stirring occasionally, until the chocolate has just melted. Remove the bowl from the pan. Set aside.
3 Meanwhile, in a large bowl, beat the butter until light and creamy. Add 150 g/5 oz icing sugar, beat until pale and fluffy. Gradually beat in the egg yolks, then the melted chocolate and vanilla essence.
4 Whisk the egg whites until they stand in soft peaks. Whisk in the remaining icing sugar and continue whisking until the mixture is stiff.

Using a large metal spoon, lightly fold the beaten egg whites into the chocolate mixture, alternately with the flour. (Fold in about 2 tablespoons of flour at a time.)
5 Pour the mixture into the prepared tin and make a shallow hollow in the centre. Bake in the oven for 50-60 minutes, until a fine warmed skewer inserted in the centre comes out clean.
6 Leave the cake to cool in the tin for 5 minutes, then turn it out on to a wire rack. Carefully peel off the

lining paper; turn the cake the right way up and leave to cool for at least 2 hours, preferably overnight.
7 When you are ready to ice, cut the cold cake horizontally in half. (Use a sharp, long-bladed knife with a serrated edge and cut with a sawing action.) Next, sieve the jam into a small saucepan; warm very gently until melted. Then remove from heat.
8 Place the top half of the cake, cut side uppermost, on a wire rack and spread with half the sieved jam. Place the other half of the cake, cut

side down, on top. Spread the top and sides with the rest of the jam.

**9** Make the icing: put the chocolate and water in a small heatproof bowl; place over a saucepan of gently simmering water and leave, stirring occasionally, until the chocolate has just melted. Remove from the heat and, using a balloon whisk, whisk in the icing sugar and glycerine until the mixture is smooth.

**10** Pour the icing over the cake and allow it to run down the sides. If necessary, dip a palette knife in hot water and use it to smooth the icing and give an even coating. Try to touch the icing as little as possible, to preserve the attractive gloss.

**11** Leave the cake in a cool place for 2-3 hours until the icing has set. [!]

---

## Cook's Notes

### ⏰ TIME
Preparing the cake mixture takes about 40 minutes; baking about 1 hour, and cooling at least 2 hours (but preferably overnight). Icing, including preparing the icing, takes 30 minutes.

### 🛍 BUYING GUIDE
Buy a really good-quality chocolate to make this luxurious cake.

You can buy small bottles of glycerine from chemist shops. It is used to prevent the icing from becoming brittle.

### 🥄 SERVING IDEAS
The Austrians like to eat Sachertorte with whipped cream.

Very much a special occasion cake, try making it for a birthday or other important family celebration.

### ❗ WATCHPOINT
Do not be tempted to chill the cake in the refrigerator, as this will make the icing lose its gloss.

### VARIATIONS
Try raspberry instead of apricot jam.

### ❓ DID YOU KNOW
This cake is traditionally decorated with the word 'Sacher' piped across the top when the icing has set.

● 460 calories/1925 kj per slice

---

### LINING THE CAKE TIN

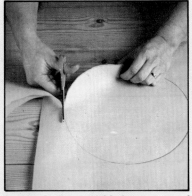

**1** Stand tin on folded greaseproof paper. Outline base. Cut out 2 circles just inside the pencil outline.

**2** Cut 2 thicknesses greaseproof strip 5 cm/2 inches deeper than tin and long enough to overlap.

**3** Make 2.5 cm/1 inch fold along 1 long edge; unfold and snip diagonally at 1 cm/½ inch intervals.

**4** Grease tin. Place circle 1 in base. Arrange strip, snipped edge down. Put circle 2 on top. Grease.

# CZECHOSLOVAKIA

A fruity, spicy flavour is characteristic of many Czech dishes, and this delicious fish recipe is no exception. *Ryba na černo* literally means fish with black sauce — because of the prunes and raisins in the dish. In Czechoslovakia, which has no sea coast, a freshwater fish such as carp would be used, but trout, much more readily available here, makes a very good substitute.

## Ryba na černo

**SERVES 4**

4 rainbow trout, each weighing about 350 g/12 oz, cleaned but heads and tails left on

COURT-BOUILLON (see Did you know)
600 ml/1 pint water
200 ml/7 fl oz wine vinegar (see Buying guide)
2 onions, sliced
1 parsnip, diced
1 carrot, diced
1 celery stalk, chopped
1 small clove garlic, chopped
1 bay leaf
½ teaspoon whole cloves
½ teaspoon ground allspice
½ teaspoon ground ginger
salt and freshly ground black pepper
bay leaves, to garnish

SAUCE
100 g/4 oz prunes, soaked if necessary, cooked for 10 minutes, stones removed and finely chopped (see Cook's tip)
50 g/2 oz seedless raisins
50 g/2 oz flaked almonds
50 g/2 oz sugar
finely grated zest and juice of ½ lemon

**1** Put all the ingredients for the *court-bouillon* into a large saucepan or fish kettle. Bring to the boil and boil gently, covered, for 15 minutes.
**2** Lower the trout carefully into the pan and turn down the heat. Cover and simmer gently for about 25 minutes, until the fish is just cooked (the flesh flakes easily when pierced with a sharp knife).
**3** Meanwhile, combine the ingredients for the sauce in a large bowl. Heat the oven to 110C/225F/Gas ¼.

## Cook's Notes

**TIME**
Preparation takes about 30 minutes, including cooking the prunes. Cooking takes about 45 minutes.

**BUYING GUIDE**
Either red or white wine vinegar gives the best flavour to the dish but malt vinegar may be used.

**DID YOU KNOW**
*Court-bouillon* is the French culinary term for the aromatic liquid in which fish, meat and vegetables are cooked. Use to add wonderful flavour to sauces.

545 calories/2300 kj per portion

**COOK'S TIP**
Cook the prunes lightly: they should still be firm when chopped.

**SERVING IDEAS**
Serve with puréed potatoes, to soak up the sauce which is basically fairly thin, despite the chunks of fruit, because no thickening agent is used. Lightly cooked cabbage, tossed in butter and sprinkled with caraway seeds, is also delicious with this piquant fish dish.
Lager is the best drink to accompany *Ryba na černo* — the sauce is too strongly flavoured to go well with wine. Czech Pils lager would be ideal.

**PREPARING FISH AND COURT-BOUILLON**

**1** *Using 2 fish slices, carefully remove the cooked trout from the large saucepan.*

**2** *Pour the court-bouillon into a fine sieve and then leave it to drain into a bowl.*

**4** Using 2 fish slices, carefully remove trout from pan (see Step 1). Place on a warmed large serving dish. Keep warm in the oven.
**5** Strain *court-bouillon* (see Step 2). Mix thoroughly with the sauce ingredients in the bowl, then return to the rinsed-out pan.

**6** Cook the sauce uncovered for 5 minutes, stirring occasionally, until heated through. Taste and adjust the seasoning, if necessary.
**7** Spoon some of the sauce over the fish, garnish with bay leaves and serve at once, with the remaining sauce handed separately.

# POLAND

*Bigos*, a slowly simmered stew of mixed game meats and sauerkraut (pickled cabbage), has been for centuries the most popular of Poland's national dishes, traditionally served on feast-days and holidays. The Poles are very fond of hunting, and in the old days a great cauldron of Bigos would hang all day over a wood fire in the forest, awaiting the return of the hungry huntsmen from the chase.

# Bigos

SERVES 4

850 g/1¾ lb mixed cooked meats
   (e.g. pork, beef, veal, chicken,
   turkey or ham), cut into 2 cm/¾
   inch cubes and 2.5 cm/1 inch
   matchsticks (see Cook's tips)
2 × 500 g/1 lb cans sauerkraut,
   chopped
600 ml/1 pint beef stock
25 g/1 oz margarine or butter
2 large onions, sliced
100 g/4 oz garlic sausage, skin
   removed and cut into 1 cm/½ inch
   cubes
50 g/2 oz dried mushrooms (see
   Buying guide), soaked and cut
   into thin strips
20 dried prunes, soaked if
   necessary, stoned and chopped
2 bay leaves
pinch of ground allspice
salt and freshly ground black pepper
½ wine glass dry red wine

**1** Put the sauerkraut with its juices into a 3-3.5 L/5¼-6 pint flameproof casserole. Stir in the beef stock and add a little water if necessary just to cover. Set the casserole over the lowest possible heat so that it is just simmering.

**2** Melt the margarine in a frying-pan, add the onions and fry gently for about 10 minutes until soft and brown. Remove the onions with a slotted spoon and stir into the sauerkraut.

**3** Add the diced meats, garlic sausage, mushrooms, prunes, bay leaves and allspice to the casserole and stir well. Season with salt and pepper.

**4** Simmer the casserole over the lowest possible heat for 2½ hours so that the flavours blend.

**5** Add the wine, taste and adjust seasoning if necessary, then stir well and simmer for a further 40 minutes until all the meats are very tender. Serve hot, straight from the casserole or refrigerate and serve hot the following day (see Serving ideas).

## Cook's Notes

### TIME
Preparation takes about 30 minutes, cooking about 3 hours.

### COOK'S TIPS
Cold cooked pheasant, duck or venison are traditionally included in Bigos, and make delicious additions if available. Some butchers and delicatessens sell smoked chicken, which would give an excellent flavour.

Cut the meats into both cube and matchstick lengths, for a varied texture.

### BUYING GUIDE
Wild mushrooms grow profusely in the Polish countryside, and are traditionally strung on to long threads in the autumn and hung up to dry from the kitchen ceiling. These would be used for making Bigos in Poland, but in this country, you can use commercially dried mushrooms, available at specialist (particularly Italian and oriental) food shops.

If you find them difficult to obtain, however, use 250 g/9 oz sliced button mushrooms fried in butter instead, and add about 1 hour before the end of cooking time. You could stir in a little mushroom ketchup as well, though nothing can replace the flavour of dried mushrooms.

### SERVING IDEAS
Serve Bigos with rye, wholemeal or French bread. Beer or vodka is best to drink with Bigos, rather than wine.

Bigos is traditionally served on the third day after cooking, having first been brought to simmering point and then allowed to cook for at least 1 hour on the 2 previous days. In between times it is stored in a cold place—ideally outdoors in a winter frost, which improves the flavour. Make Bigos at least the day before, if you can.

●615 calories/2575 kj per portion

The word *gefilte* is a Yiddish word, meaning 'stuffed', and this dish probably originated among the Jewish population in Poland. The mixture of chopped fish, onions and other ingredients would have been served in a large filleted fish like carp or bream, but gradually it became popular to serve the minced fish mixture as individual balls. This is the way gefilte fish is served today, particularly at Passover and other similar Jewish celebrations.

# Gefilte fish

**MAKES 12-14 FISH BALLS**

500 g/1 lb haddock (see Buying
   guide)
225-275 g/8-10 oz hake
225 g/8 oz halibut (see Economy)
275 g/10 oz herring
225 g/8 oz onions
225 g/8 oz carrots, sliced
salt and freshly ground black
   pepper
600 ml/1 pint cold water
2 eggs, lightly beaten
100 g/4 oz medium matzo meal (see
   Buying guide)
25 g/1 oz ground almonds
   (optional)
1 teaspoon sugar (optional)

**1** Remove fish heads and tails and
discard. Fillet and skin fish and put
the bones and skin into the bottom
of a large saucepan. Skin the onions
and place skin in the pan with fish
skin and bones.
**2** Add sliced carrots, salt and black
pepper. Pour on the water and
bring to boil. Lower heat and
simmer, covered, for 30 minutes,
then remove from heat. Put to one
side in a warm place.
**3** Mince or finely chop the fish and
onions, using a mincer or food
processor. ☐ Place minced fish
in a mixing bowl.
**4** Add the eggs, matzo meal,
ground almonds and sugar, if
using. Season very generously and
mix everything together thoroughly.
Carefully roll the mixture into
slightly flattish balls, about 6.5 cm/
2½ inches across (see Steps).
**5** Gently slide the balls into the
liquid in the pan of fish stock.
Return to the heat and cook,
covered, on a low heat for 1 hour
(see Cook's tip).
**6** Leave the fish balls in the pan to
cool and then remove carefully with
a slotted spoon. Place the fish on a
serving dish, overlapping them
slightly. Arrange a piece of cooked
carrot on top of each piece of fish.
**7** Strain the cooking liquid into a
jug. Put both the gefilte fish and
the strained cooking liquid in the
refrigerator and chill for 1 hour.
Serve cold (see Serving ideas).

## Cook's Notes

### TIME
Preparation takes about
30 minutes. Cooking
takes about 1½ hours. Allow at
least 2 hours for cooling and
chilling in the refrigerator.

### BUYING GUIDE
This is a traditional
gefilte fish mixture, a
blend of haddock, hake, halibut
and herring – a three to one
proportion of dry white and
rich oily fish. It is possible to
substitute another fish mixture
according to preference or
availability. Bream and whiting,
for example, make a very good
substitute for the haddock and
hake. Or buy fillets and ask
your fishmonger for some skin
and bones to use in making the
cooking stock.
   You should be able to buy
matzo meal at most super-
markets, but finely crushed
water biscuits or matzo crackers
can be used instead.

### VARIATIONS
The same mixture can
be used to make fried
fish balls, which are a popular
alternative to boiled ones: fry
the balls in hot shallow oil for
about 7 minutes on each side,
until they are quite brown. Or
make much smaller balls and
deep-fry them in oil. These
make excellent cocktail snacks,
served on sticks with a sweet
and sour dipping sauce.

### COOK'S TIP
Check liquid during
cooking time and, if
necessary, add a little more
water to prevent pan burning.

### ECONOMY
Halibut can often be
expensive; ask for flap
or a similar inexpensive cut.

### DID YOU KNOW
Matzo meal is made
from matzos, the crisp
unleavened bread which is
eaten at Passover, during which
period leavened bread is strictly
forbidden.

### SERVING IDEAS
Boiled gefilte fish is
almost always served
cold, accompanied by its own
sauce and by a special, very hot
piquant sauce known as *chrane*,
a horseradish and beetroot relish
available ready-made in jars
from Jewish delicatessens.
   Fried gefilte fish is good hot
or cold, served either with
*chrane*, or mayonnaise.
   Serve either boiled or fried
gefilte as an hors d'oeuvre, or as
a main course with salads.

### WATCHPOINT
Do not mince fish too
finely – an electric food
processor can reduce fish to a
purée if you are not careful.

● 135 calories/575 kj per fish ball

### SHAPING THE FISH BALLS

**1** Add more matzo meal if the
mixture is too liquid to make into
firm balls. Stir well to mix.

**2** Using slightly wet hands, roll
the mixture into 12-14 flattened
balls, 6.5 cm/2½ inches across.

# HUNGARY

A *paprikas* (pronounced 'paprikash') is a very popular Hungarian dish made with pork, veal, lamb or chicken, sweet paprika and lots of soured cream. *Paprikas* is traditionally served with dumplings called *nockerln*, and together they make a tasty meal.

# Pork paprikas

SERVES 4-6

1 kg/2 lb stewing pork, trimmed of excess fat and cut into 2 cm/¾ inch cubes (see Buying guide)
2 tablespoons lard or vegetable oil
500 g/1 lb onions, sliced
1 clove garlic, finely chopped (optional)
1 tablespoon sweet paprika
salt
150 ml/¼ pint water
1 green pepper, deseeded and sliced
1 red pepper, deseeded and sliced
250 g/9 oz tomatoes, skinned and sliced
300 ml/½ pint soured cream

1 Melt the lard in a large, heavy-based saucepan or flameproof casserole. Add the onions and garlic, if using, and fry gently for 5-10 minutes, until the onions are soft and lightly coloured. Remove with a slotted spoon and drain on absorbent paper.
2 Stir in the paprika and cook gently for 1 minute. [!]
3 Add about one-quarter of the pork cubes to the pan and cook quickly, stirring, over moderate heat until lightly coloured. Remove the pork from the pan, set aside with the onions and cook the remaining pork cubes in the same way, in 3 more batches.
4 Return the pork and onions to the pan. Season to taste with salt, add the water and bring to the boil. Lower the heat, cover the pan tightly and simmer for 1 hour.
5 Add the peppers and tomatoes to the pan and simmer for a further 30 minutes. ✳
6 Beat the soured cream with a fork until smooth. Reserve 75-150 ml/ 3-5 fl oz and stir remainder into the pan (see Cook's tip). Heat gently, stirring, but do not allow to boil or the cream will separate. Taste and adjust seasoning and serve at once with the reserved cream swirled on top or handed separately in a jug. Accompany the pork paprikas with a dish of hot nockerln.

# Nockerln

SERVES 4-6
225 g/8 oz plain flour
salt and freshly ground black pepper
175 ml/6 fl oz soda water (see Cook's tip) [!]
25 g/1 oz butter, to finish

1 Sift the flour into a large bowl and season with plenty of salt and pepper. Bring a large saucepan of salted water to the boil.
2 Very gradually add the soda water to the flour, mixing with a fork until the dough is a soft but not sticky consistency.
3 Drop teaspoons of the dough into the boiling water (see Step). When the dumplings rise to the surface, cook for about 5 minutes. [!] Drain the dumplings thoroughly in a colander.

4 Melt the butter in a saucepan. Add the drained dumplings and carefully turn them to coat with the butter.
5 Pile the dumplings into a warmed serving dish and serve with the Pork paprikas.

## COOKING NOCKERLN

*Drop 1 teaspoon of the dough into the boiling water, immersing the spoon to make scooping up of the next portion of dough easier.*

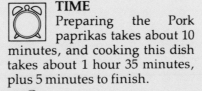

*Cook's Notes*

**Pork paprikas**

 **TIME**
Preparing the Pork paprikas takes about 10 minutes, and cooking this dish takes about 1 hour 35 minutes, plus 5 minutes to finish.

**BUYING GUIDE**
Thick end of belly, which has a higher proportion of lean meat to fat than the flank end, is a good cut for this dish. Belly of pork gives a very tender result and is considerably less expensive then either fillet or tenderloin of pork.

**COOK'S TIP**
Always beat soured cream before adding to a hot dish, as this helps to give a smoother finish.

**[!] WATCHPOINT**
It is important to heat the paprika to release its full flavour, but do be sure to keep the heat low as it will burn easily if overheated at this stage.

**✳ FREEZING**
The paprikas freezes well without the cream. Prepare to the end of stage 5, transfer to a rigid container, cool quickly, then seal, label and freeze for up to 3 months. To serve: defrost at room temperature, then gently heat through on top of the cooker until bubbling. Finish as in stage 6.

● 530 calories/2230 kj per portion

**Nockerln**

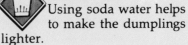 **TIME**
The nockerln take about 15 minutes to prepare and cook.

**COOK'S TIP**
Using soda water helps to make the dumplings lighter.

**[!] WATCHPOINT**
Do not overcook the dumplings or they will harden.

● 250 calories/1050 kj per portion

ITALY

Veal is Italy's favourite meat, and there is a vast range of Italian veal recipes. *Osso buco,* braised shin of veal, is especially popular: the marrow in the centre of the bones is considered a great delicacy. *Osso buco,* which originated in Lombardy in northern Italy, is one of Italy's great classic dishes, but it is particularly associated with Milan where it is traditionally served with *Risotto alla Milanese* – rice cooked with dry white wine, chicken stock and butter and sprinkled with Parmesan cheese.

# Osso buco

SERVES 4

4 slices shin of veal, about 6.5 cm/
  2½ inches thick and each
  weighing about 300 g/10 oz (see
  Buying guide)
2 tablespoons plain flour
salt and freshly ground black pepper
50 g/2 oz butter
2 tablespoons olive oil
1 onion, finely chopped
1 small carrot, finely chopped
1 celery stalk, finely chopped
150 ml/¼ pint dry white wine
400 g/14 oz can tomatoes
2 tablespoons tomato purée
1 bay leaf
¼ teaspoon dried sage
¼ teaspoon sugar

TO FINISH
1 clove garlic, finely chopped
finely grated zest of ½ lemon
2 tablespoons finely chopped fresh
  parsley

1 Firmly tie each piece of veal in 2 places with thin string so that it will keep in a neat shape during cooking. Spread the flour out on a flat plate, season with salt and pepper and turn the veal in the seasoned flour, to coat thoroughly.
2 Heat half the butter and oil in a large shallow flameproof casserole, add the veal and fry quickly, turning it until browned all over. Drain the veal well over the casserole, then transfer to a large plate and set aside.
3 Heat the remaining butter and oil in the casserole, add the onion,

carrot and celery and fry gently for 5 minutes, stirring occasionally, until onion is soft and lightly coloured.
4 Pour the wine into the casserole and simmer, uncovered, for 8-10 minutes until reduced by half. Stir in the tomatoes with their juice and the tomato purée. Add the bay leaf, sage and sugar. Stir well and season with salt and pepper. Bring slowly to the boil, stirring constantly.
5 Return the veal to the casserole, making sure that the bones are upright, to prevent the marrow from falling out during cooking. Cover closely with a lid and simmer gently for 1½-2 hours or until the veal is very tender (the meat should be almost falling from the bones).
6 Meanwhile, mix finishing ingredients together in a small bowl.
7 Sprinkle finishing mixture over the veal 3-4 minutes before serving and spoon the sauce over the veal, keeping veal upright, to distribute the flavour. Remove string and serve hot, straight from the casserole (see Serving ideas).

## Cook's Notes

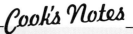

**TIME**
Preparation takes about 30 minutes, cooking about 2 hours.

**BUYING GUIDE**
Order the shin of veal well in advance from the butcher. Slices are cut across the leg and should be as meaty as possible, and must include the bone complete with the marrow in the centre.

**SERVING IDEAS**
Serve with risotto or buttered noodles.

**DID YOU KNOW**
The finish of garlic, lemon zest and parsley gives *osso buco* its essential Milanese touch. The finish is called *gremolata* in Italian.

In Italy, some restaurants provide a special marrow fork or spoon to scoop out every last bit of marrow from the centre of the bones.

●450 calories/1900 kj per portion

# SPAIN

*Paella,* a wonderfully tasty mixture of saffron rice, meat, fish and vegetables, must be Spain's most famous dish. You can ring endless changes on the ingredients: the recipe given here—using chicken, pork, spicy sausage and shellfish—is just one version.

The only essential ingredients for every paella are long-grain rice, olive oil and saffron.

The beauty of paella is that it can be simple or elaborate, and the ingredients varied to suit your pocket as well as your taste.

You can serve it for a simple summer lunch, or dress it up as a more elaborate, but easy-to-prepare party dish. Paella is perfect for a buffet, as it can so easily be eaten with a fork.

## Paella

SERVES 6

12 unshelled mussels, defrosted if frozen (see Steps), or 150 g/
  5 oz can or jar mussels, drained
1 kg/2 lb chicken, cut into 8 pieces
100 g/4 oz lean pork fillet, cut into 1
  cm/½ inch cubes
salt and freshly ground black pepper
100 ml/3½ fl oz olive oil
2 raw chorizo sausages, cut into 5
  mm/¼ inch slices
1 onion, finely chopped
2 cloves garlic, crushed (optional)
1 red pepper, deseeded and cut into
  4 cm × 5 mm/1½ × ¼ inch strips
250 g/9 oz tomatoes, skinned,
  deseeded and finely chopped
1 teaspoon sweet paprika
500 g/1 lb long-grain rice
½ teaspoon saffron strands,
  crushed and soaked for 2 hours in
  1 L/1¾ pints boiling hot chicken
  stock
250 g/9 oz cooked unpeeled prawns,
  defrosted if frozen (see Buying
  guide), or 100 g/4 oz peeled
  prawns, defrosted if frozen, or
  200 g/7 oz can peeled prawns,
  drained
400 g/14 oz can artichoke hearts,
  drained
225 g/8 oz frozen peas, defrosted

1 If using unshelled mussels, prepare them as shown in the Steps.
2 Cook the prepared mussels: rinse the soaked mussels thoroughly, then drain. Pour 150 ml/¼ pint water into a heavy frying-pan large enough to hold the mussels in a single layer. Add the mussels, cover and bring to the boil then lower the heat and simmer for 5-6 minutes, shaking the pan gently once or twice. If the mussels have not opened, cook for 1-2 minutes longer. Discard any unopened mussels ⟨!⟩ and set the rest aside.
3 Season the chicken pieces and pork cubes with salt and pepper. Heat half the oil in a paella pan (see Did you know), large frying-pan, or large, shallow flameproof casserole. Add the chicken and pork and fry over moderate heat for 10-15 minutes, turning frequently, until browned on all sides. After 5 minutes cooking, add the sausage slices to the pan and turn to brown. With a slotted spoon, lift out the meats on to a plate and set aside.
4 Heat the remaining oil in the pan. Add the onion, garlic, if using, pepper strips and chopped tomatoes and cook over gentle heat for about 5 minutes, stirring from time to time, until the onion is soft and the mixture well blended. Stir in the paprika. Cook for 1 minute. Remove from heat. Stir in rice.
5 Strain the saffron stock into the pan and stir once. Bring to the boil and cook for 5 minutes.
6 Arrange the chicken, pork, sausages, cooked mussels, prawns and artichoke hearts on top of the rice. Sprinkle over the peas.
7 Turn down heat to low. Cook for 12-15 minutes, until rice is tender and all liquid absorbed.
8 Turn off the heat under the pan. Cover the pan with a lid or drape it with a kitchen towel. Leave for 3-4 minutes, to allow the flavours to blend. Serve straight from the pan.

## TO CLEAN MUSSELS

1 *Check mussels are really fresh: tap any open ones against work surface. Discard if they do not shut.*

2 *Pull away any beards (pieces of hanging seaweed gripped between the 2 shells of the mussel).*

3 *Scrub mussels under cold running water, then scrape away encrustations with a sharp knife. Then soak mussels in fresh cold water to cover for 2-3 hours. Change the water several times.*

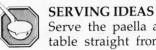

## Cooks Notes

### TIME
Preparation takes about 1¼ hours if using un-shelled mussels. Allow a further 2-3 hours for soaking the mussels and saffron threads. Cooking the paella takes about 45 minutes.

### WATCHPOINT
It is absolutely vital to discard any unopened mussels—this shows they are not fresh, which can cause serious food poisoning.

### BUYING GUIDE
Try to buy mussels and prawns in the shell, as they look so attractive in the finished dish. Both are available from high-quality fishmongers, and frozen from freezer centres and some supermarkets.

### SERVING IDEAS
Serve the paella at the table straight from the pan, as the Spaniards do.

The paella is usually eaten by itself—a vegetable accompaniment is not necessary.

### VARIATIONS
In Spain, paella is often made with rabbit, and this could be substituted for chicken.

For a special occasion, add some lobster meat to the paella.

### DID YOU KNOW
The name paella comes from *paellera*, the pan in which the dish is traditionally cooked in Spain: it is shallow with gently sloping sides and 2 flattened handles. You can buy special paella pans from high-quality kitchen equipment shops or departments of big stores—or, better still, buy one on holiday in Spain. But if you do not have a *paellera*, a large heavy frying-pan, preferably with a lid, or a large, shallow flameproof casserole will do very well instead for making the paella.

●980 calories/4100 kj per portion

**This is a very old traditional dish from southern Spain, typical of Andalusia and La Mancha. There are many regional variations, some with very little liquid and some without tomatoes; olive oil and red wine vinegar, however, are always included.**

Originally a midday meal, gazpacho was prepared on the spot in a wooden bowl and eaten with wooden spoons by workers in the fields. This sophisticated modern version makes a wonderfully refreshing cold vegetable soup in summer, when cucumbers, tomatoes and green peppers are at their best. The soup is served in individual bowls with garnishes of croutons, hard-boiled eggs, cucumber, peppers and onion.

## Gazpacho

**SERVES 4**

500 g/1 lb tomatoes, skinned and coarsely chopped
½ cucumber, peeled and coarsely chopped
1 green pepper, deseeded and coarsely chopped
1 small onion, coarsely chopped
1 clove garlic, chopped
2 slices white bread, crusts removed, crumbled
1 teaspoon salt, or to taste
2 tablespoons red wine vinegar
1 L/1¾ pints iced water
5 tablespoons olive oil

**TO SERVE**

2 slices bread, crusts removed, cubed
4 tablespoons olive oil
2 eggs, hard-boiled and chopped
½ cucumber, peeled and finely chopped
1 small green pepper, deseeded and finely chopped
1 onion, finely diced (see Steps)

**1** In a large bowl, combine the tomatoes, cucumber, green pepper, onion, garlic, bread, salt and vinegar. Add the water and mix thoroughly (see Cook's tip). Purée the mixture in a food processor or blender until smooth. Return the purée to the bowl and whisk in the oil in a thin, steady stream. Cover the bowl with cling film and refrigerate for about 2 hours until thoroughly chilled.

**2** To make the croûtons: heat the oil in a heavy frying-pan over moderate heat until very hot, add the bread cubes and fry until golden brown on all sides, turning them frequently. Drain on absorbent paper and put into a small serving bowl.

**3** Put the eggs, cucumber, green pepper and onion into separate small serving bowls.

**4** When the soup is well chilled, stir thoroughly ☐ and taste and adjust seasoning. Pour into 4 chilled individual soup bowls and hand the garnishes separately.

### Cook's Notes

**TIME**
Preparation takes about 45 minutes, but remember that the soup needs to be chilled for about 2 hours.

**WATCHPOINT**
Do not forget to stir the soup just before serving.

**COOK'S TIP**
If the tomatoes have a poor colour, add some tomato purée to the ingredients before you purée them.

●370 calories/1550 kj per portion

### HOW TO DICE ONIONS

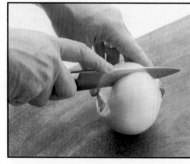

**1** Peel the onion and cut it in half lengthways with a sharp knife on a chopping board.

**2** Place the onion with the cut side down. Slice the onion horizontally, leaving the root end uncut.

**3** Cut the onion lengthways, again leaving the root end uncut.

**4** Now cut across the onion, which will fall into tiny dice.

*Tortilla española* or *tortilla de patatas,* the famous Spanish omelette made with fried potatoes and onions, is quite different from a French folded omelette, because it is flat and is cooked on both sides for considerably longer. In Spain it's usually served hot or cold as a first course, and is also eaten cold as a snack, cut into cubes. As a lunch or supper main course, it may be accompanied by slices of spicy sausage and a fresh tomato sauce.

# Tortilla española

SERVES 2-4
4 large eggs, beaten
4 tablespoons olive oil (see Cook's tips)
2 onions, total weight about 175 g/6 oz, finely chopped
3 potatoes, total weight about 350 g/12 oz, cut into 1 cm/½ inch dice (see Buying guide)
salt and freshly ground black pepper
olives and sweet pepper rings, to garnish (optional)

1 Heat 3 tablespoons of the oil in a large, heavy-based frying-pan (see Cook's tips). Add onions and potatoes, cover the pan and cook over moderate heat, stirring occasionally, for about 15 minutes, until the onions and potatoes are soft and golden. ⚠

2 Remove the vegetables from the pan with a slotted spoon, transfer to a large plate and set aside to cool for 5 minutes.

3 Wipe out the pan thoroughly with absorbent paper.

4 Season the beaten eggs with salt and pepper and stir the cooled onions and potatoes into the eggs.

5 Heat the remaining oil in the pan, add the egg and vegetable mixture and cook, uncovered, over moderate heat for 12-15 minutes until the base is set but the centre of the omelette is still slightly creamy.

6 Run a spatula round the edge of the omelette and remove the pan from the heat. Invert a large round plate over the pan (see Cook's tips and Step 1), then holding the pan and plate firmly together, invert the pan and carefully turn the omelette on to the plate.

*Cook's Notes*

 **TIME**
Preparation and cooking take about 45 minutes.

 **COOK'S TIPS**
Olive oil is essential for the right flavour.

A heavy cast-iron frying-pan, kept specially for making omelettes and wiped, not washed, after use, is ideal, but a non-stick frying-pan may also be used. The pan must have a lid, and should be 20-23 cm/ 8-9 inches in diameter.

In Spain, many cooks use a special plate with a handle attached which makes it easier to turn the omelette over (see photograph). This omelette turner can be bought in most pottery shops in Spain, and is well worth looking out for if you are on holiday there.

 **WATCHPOINT**
The vegetables should be fried until soft and golden, but they must not be allowed to brown.

**BUYING GUIDE**
Choose waxy potatoes, such as Maris Peer, which keep their shape better than floury ones when cut into small dice.

**SERVING IDEAS**
The omelette is good eaten hot, warm or cold. The quantities in this recipe will serve 4 for a starter or 2 for a main course.

The cold omelette, cut into wedges, makes an unusual addition to a picnic basket.

●550 calories/2300 kj as starter

---

**HOW TO TURN THE OMELETTE**

**1** *Invert plate over pan, then holding pan and plate together, invert pan and turn omelette on to plate.*

**2** *Carefully slip the omelette back into the pan, browned side uppermost. Allow base to brown.*

7 Carefully slip the omelette back into the pan (see Step 2), browned side uppermost. Cook over moderate heat for a further 3-5 minutes, until the underside is browned.

8 Slide the omelette on to a warmed round serving plate and garnish with olives and sweet pepper rings, if liked. Serve the omelette cut into wedges (see Serving ideas).

# GREECE

Moussaka, a spicy dish of minced meat, aubergines and tomatoes baked with a delicious savoury topping, is one of the most popular main-course choices in Greek homes and restaurants. In fact, there are few better ways of conjuring up the atmosphere of a Greek taverna than by serving Moussaka with salad and a bottle of Greek wine.

## Moussaka

SERVES 6

500 g/1 lb lean minced lamb or beef
1 kg/2 lb aubergines, cut into
 1 cm/½ inch slices
salt
about 225 ml/8 fl oz sunflower-seed
 oil (see Watchpoints)
500 g/1 lb onions, thinly sliced
2 cloves garlic, cut into slivers
750 g/1½ lb tomatoes, skinned and
 sliced
2 tablespoons beef stock
½ teaspoon dried basil
freshly ground black pepper
250 g/9 oz Gruyère or Cheddar
 cheese, thinly sliced
2 tablespoons chopped parsley

TOPPING
15 g/½ oz butter
15 g/½ oz plain flour
300 ml/½ pint milk
2 eggs, separated
pinch of freshly grated nutmeg

1 Put the sliced aubergines in a colander and sprinkle them with salt, turning to coat evenly. Set the colander on a plate and leave to drain for 30 minutes.

2 Heat about 50 ml/2 fl oz oil in a large, heavy-based frying-pan. Add the onions and garlic and fry over moderate heat, stirring occasionally for about 15 minutes, until golden. Remove from the pan with a slotted spoon, drain on absorbent paper and set aside.

3 Heat a further 25 ml/1 fl oz oil in the pan. Add the minced lamb and fry gently, stirring often to remove any lumps, for 5-10 minutes until the meat has lost all its pinkness. Remove the mince from the pan with a slotted spoon, drain on absorbent paper and set aside with the onions.

4 Rinse the aubergines under cold running water and pat dry with absorbent paper.

5 Heat a further 50 ml/2 fl oz oil in the pan, add the aubergines and fry over moderate heat, turning occasionally, for 10-15 minutes until golden on both sides. Add more oil as necessary. Drain the fried aubergines thoroughly on absorbent paper.

6 Meanwhile, put the tomatoes in a saucepan, add the beef stock and basil and season with salt and pepper. Cook over gentle heat, stirring occasionally with a wooden spoon for 10-15 minutes, to make a thick, pulpy sauce.

7 Heat the oven to 180C/350F/Gas 4.

8 Brush a 30 × 20 × 5 cm/12 × 8 × 2 inch baking dish with oil. In the dish, make layers of aubergines, cheese, minced lamb and onions, seasoning the layers with salt and pepper and moistening with the tomato sauce. Repeat until all the ingredients are used.

9 Make the topping: melt the butter in a saucepan, sprinkle in the flour and stir over low heat until straw-coloured. Remove from the heat and gradually stir in the milk. Return to the heat and simmer, stirring, until thickened and smooth. Remove from heat and allow to cool slightly. Beat in the egg yolks and a pinch of nutmeg. Whisk the egg whites until soft peaks form, then fold lightly into the sauce mixture.

10 Pour the topping over the dish and bake in the oven for about 1 hour, until the topping is browned. Remove from oven and sprinkle with the parsley. Serve hot, straight from the dish.

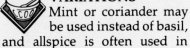

### Cook's Notes

**TIME**
Preparation, including pre-cooking and draining the aubergines, takes about 1 hour; cooking, 1 hour.

**SERVING IDEAS**
Accompany moussaka with a salad and a loaf of Greek bread, with Greek pastries to follow.
 Serve with a popular Greek wine such as *retsina*, or a full-bodied red Othello.

**WATCHPOINTS**
Aubergines soak up oil like blotting paper, so have extra ready to add to the pan if it shows signs of becoming dry.
 Draining on absorbent paper is essential, otherwise the finished dish will be too oily.

**VARIATIONS**
Mint or coriander may be used instead of basil, and allspice is often used in place of the grated nutmeg.
 Thinly sliced, par-fried potatoes may be added with the aubergines, or courgettes may be substituted for aubergines.
 In Greece, natural yoghurt is often used to thicken the topping mixture, or it may be flavoured with Greek cheese, such as shredded Haloumi. In this case, omit the other cheese from the layers.

● 800 calories/3350 kj per portion

Lamb is the most popular meat in Greece, where the hilly countryside is better suited to grazing sheep than cattle. The Greeks cook lamb in a variety of ways—roasted on a spit or grilled over charcoal. Here the succulent, tender meat is cooked on top of the stove and served in a tangy egg and lemon sauce.

Accompanied by a simple pilaff of rice and a salad of lettuce and tomato, Avgolemono lamb is a great favourite with Greek families. Try it for a summer meal, and bring some of the atmosphere of a sunny Greek island to your table. To drink with the lamb, serve chilled Retsina, the Greek white wine with pine resin added, which gives it a distinctive smoky taste. Retsina is now available from chain wine stores.

## Avgolemono lamb

SERVES 4
750 g/1½ lb boneless leg of lamb, cut into 2.5 cm/1 inch cubes
25 g/1 oz margarine or butter
1 large onion, chopped
4 celery stalks, chopped
1 tablespoon chopped fresh dill or 1 teaspoon dried dillweed
600 ml/1 pint vegetable or light chicken stock
salt and freshly ground black pepper
2 small firm hearts of round lettuce, cut into quarters (see Cook's tips)
4 teaspoons cornflour
2 egg yolks
2 tablespoons lemon juice
2 tablespoons chopped parsley
lemon wedges, to garnish

1 Melt the margarine in a large heavy-based saucepan. Add the onion and cook gently for about 5 minutes until soft and lightly coloured. Add the lamb, increase heat and stir until meat is sealed but not browned (see Cook's tips).
2 Add the celery, the dill and stock to the pan and season to taste with salt and pepper. Bring to the boil, cover, lower heat and simmer for 1 hour. ✳
3 Heat oven to 110C/225F/Gas ¼.

4 Put the lettuce in a colander, pour over boiling water and drain well. Add the lettuce to the pan, cover and simmer for 15 minutes.
5 Strain off the cooking liquid from the lamb into a clean saucepan. Keep the meat and vegetables warm in the oven.
6 To make the sauce: in a small bowl, mix the cornflour to a smooth paste with a little water. Heat the cooking liquid in the saucepan and when boiling add the cornflour paste and cook over moderate heat, stirring constantly, until the sauce is thickened and smooth. Lower the heat and simmer for 2 minutes.
7 Meanwhile, beat the egg yolks in a large bowl until creamy. Whisk in the lemon juice, a little at a time, until it is all incorporated. Gradually stir the hot sauce into the egg and lemon mixture in the bowl, !beating well until thoroughly blended. Return to the pan and reheat gently, stirring, without allowing it to boil. Taste and adjust the seasoning, if necessary.
8 Arrange the lamb and vegetables on a warmed serving dish and pour over the sauce. Sprinkle with the parsley, garnish with the lemon wedges and serve at once.

## Greek pilaff

SERVES 4
50 g/2 oz margarine or butter
1 onion, finely chopped
175 g/6 oz long-grain rice
500 ml/18 fl oz chicken stock
50 g/2 oz black olives, stoned and chopped

1 Melt the margarine in a saucepan, add the onion and fry gently until soft but not coloured. Add the rice

and stir gently over moderate heat for 2 minutes, until the grains are thoroughly coated. ! Pour in the stock, stir to mix and bring to the boil. Stir once, cover and simmer gently for about 20 minutes, or until the rice is tender and fluffy and all the stock is absorbed. !
2 Fork in the chopped olives, cover pan and leave for 3 minutes. Serve at once (see Serving ideas).

## Avgolemono lamb

 **TIME**
Preparation takes about 20 minutes. Cooking takes about 1½ hours.

 **COOK'S TIPS**
Use the outside lettuce leaves to make a salad to accompany the dish.

'Sealing' the meat ensures that the flavour and juices do not escape during cooking.

**SERVING IDEAS**
Serve the dish with Greek pilaff (see recipe), pitta bread, and a salad of shredded lettuce and sliced tomatoes and onion.

**⚠ WATCHPOINT**
It is important to add the hot sauce gradually to the uncooked beaten egg yolks, whisking all the time, and to reheat very gently to avoid curdling.

**✳ FREEZING**
Prepare the recipe up to the end of stage 2. Transfer to a rigid container, cool, seal and label. Freeze for up to 6 months. To serve: transfer to a large saucepan and reheat gently from frozen on top of the cooker, until heated right through. Complete from stage 3.

●520 calories/2175 kj per portion

## Greek pilaff

**TIME**
Preparation and pre-cooking 5 minutes, simmering rice, 20 minutes.

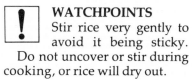 **SERVING IDEAS**
Press the cooked pilaff into an oiled 850 ml/ 1½ pint mould, or into individual moulds or coffee cups, then turn out on to a serving dish.

**⚠ WATCHPOINTS**
Stir rice very gently to avoid it being sticky.
Do not uncover or stir during cooking, or rice will dry out.

●270 calories/1125 kj per portion

# TURKEY

*Imam bayildi,* a Turkish dish of fragrantly stuffed aubergines, means literally 'the priest fainted', the legend being that a certain *imam* or priest overdid the helpings and promptly passed out from a surfeit of pleasure. Other versions say that the *imam* fainted when he heard the cost of the dish because of the amount of oil used in making it. Traditionally, olive oil is used, but for the sake of economy, we have substituted sunflower-seed oil.

*Imam bayildi* is a delicious starter which is eaten cold. Although it can be served the same day it is made, the flavour improves considerably if the dish is left overnight.

*Imam bayildi* is quite filling, so serve a light main course to follow.

# Imam bayildi

**SERVES 6**

4 aubergines, each weighing about 175 g/6 oz (see Buying guide)
salt
150-300 ml/¼-½ pint sunflower-seed oil (see Watchpoint)
500 g/1 lb onions, finely chopped
4 cloves garlic, finely sliced
50 g/2 oz currants
freshly ground black pepper
pinch of ground allspice
750 g/1½ lb large tomatoes, skinned and chopped (see Buying guide)
bunch of fresh parsley, finely chopped
3-4 bay leaves
sprig of fresh thyme, or ½ teaspoon dried thyme
lettuce leaves or flat-leaved parsley, and lemon wedges, to garnish (optional)

**1** Wipe the aubergines with a damp cloth and trim off the stalks. Cut each aubergine in half lengthways, then score the flesh with a knife and sprinkle with salt (see Steps).
**2** Put the aubergines, cut side up, in a colander, cover with a plate and weight down with a 2 kg/4½ lb weight (see Cook's tip). Leave for 2 hours to draw out the bitter juices.

## HOW TO PREPARE AUBERGINES

**1** *Wipe the aubergines with a damp cloth. Then, using a sharp knife, trim off the stalks and cut each aubergine in half lengthways. Score the flesh of the aubergine and sprinkle it evenly all over with salt.*

**2** *Put the aubergines in a colander, cut side up, and set over a saucepan. Cover with a plate and weight down with a 2 kg/4½ lb weight or with flour or sugar bags or cans. Leave for 2 hours to draw out the bitter juices.*

**3** Rinse the aubergines under cold running water and pat dry with absorbent paper. ⚠ Then, using a small knife, scoop out the flesh taking care not to damage the skin.
**4** Heat 150 ml/¼ pint oil in a large frying-pan, add the onions and garlic and fry gently for 5 minutes until the onions are soft and lightly coloured.
**5** Meanwhile, put the currants in a bowl and cover with boiling water. Leave to swell for 1-2 minutes.
**6** Add the aubergine flesh to the frying-pan, with salt and pepper to taste. Drain the currants, if necessary, then stir into the aubergine mixture with the allspice.
**7** Add the chopped tomato flesh and parsley to the aubergine mixture, stir well to mix, then cook for 10-15 minutes, stirring constantly. Add more oil if the mixture becomes dry.

**8** Meanwhile, heat the oven to 170C/325F/Gas 3.
**9** Remove the mixture from the heat, taste and adjust seasoning.
**10** Put the aubergine skins close together in an ovenproof dish and spoon in the cooked stuffing. Any surplus mixture can be pressed in alongside the shells. Crumble the bay leaves over the top and sprinkle over the thyme.
**11** Bake in the oven for about 1¼ hours or until the aubergines' skins are cooked and look translucent.
**12** Leave to cool in the oil, then cover and refrigerate overnight, still in the oil.
**13** Remove the dish from the refrigerator 2 hours before serving to take the chill off. Serve cold, arranged on a serving platter, garnished with lettuce or parsley and lemon wedges, if liked. Serve any extra stuffing in a bowl.

## Cook's Notes

**TIME**
For best results make *imam bayildi* the day before it is needed and allow for cooling and overnight chilling in the refrigerator. Draining the aubergines takes 2 hours, preparation 40 minutes and cooking about 1¼ hours.

**WATCHPOINT**
Aubergines have an infinite capacity for absorbing oil, so make sure you have more oil handy in case.
The juice stains so avoid contact with your clothes.

**BUYING GUIDE**
You will need long aubergines rather than the more rounded ones.
Large continental tomatoes are particularly good in this recipe because they have more flavour.

**COOK'S TIP**
If you do not have kitchen scale weights, use bags of flour or sugar or some heavy cans to weight down the aubergines.

**SERVING IDEAS**
Serve with hot pitta bread for scooping up the filling.

● 375 calories/1575 kj per portion

# ISRAEL

*Falafel* – small, spicy rissoles made from chick-peas – have been adopted as one of Israel's favourite national dishes, although in fact they originated in Egypt as *ta'amia*, patties made from dried white beans. Falafel are eaten on many occasions – as a snack dipped into natural yoghurt or hummus, for lunch with a variety of salads, or even for breakfast. They are sold in cafés and by street vendors as an Israeli version of 'fast food', and may be tucked into a pocket of pitta bread for easy eating.

# Falafel

MAKES ABOUT 20
**250 g/9 oz dried chick-peas, soaked overnight (see Buying guide)**
**1 large onion, finely grated**
**4 tablespoons fresh parsley, finely chopped**
**1 clove garlic, crushed**
**1 teaspoon ground coriander**
**1 teaspoon ground cumin**
**good pinch of chilli powder**
**salt and freshly ground black pepper**
**olive oil, for frying**
**a little plain flour, for dusting**

TO GARNISH
**coriander leaves**
**lemon wedges**

**1** Drain the chick-peas and rinse under cold running water. Put them in a large saucepan and cover with fresh cold water. Bring to the boil, then lower the heat and simmer for at least 1 hour, until very tender, adding more boiling water to the pan if necessary. Drain thoroughly.
**2** Pass the chick-peas through a vegetable mill or mincer, then transfer to a bowl and mash with a fork to make a smooth, thick purée. Or work the chick-peas in a blender or food processor until puréed.
**3** Stir in the onion together with the parsley, garlic, coriander, cumin and chilli. Season to taste with salt and pepper. Cover and refrigerate for at least 1 hour.
**4** Heat the oven to 110C/225F/Gas ¼.
**5** Scoop up tablespoons of the mixture and, with floured hands, shape

into flat cakes 2.5 cm/1 inch across.
**6** Heat 2 tablespoons olive oil in a large frying-pan, add one-third of the falafel and fry gently  for about 5 minutes, turning once very carefully with a fish slice, until brown and crisp. Drain well on absorbent paper and transfer to a warmed serving dish. Keep warm in the oven while frying the remainder in 2 batches, adding more olive oil as needed. Drain on absorbent paper, arrange with the other falafel on the serving dish and garnish with coriander leaves and lemon wedges. Serve at once (see Serving ideas).

## Cook's Notes

**TIME**
Cooking the chick-peas takes about 1 hour; making the purée takes about 2-3 minutes in a food processor, about 10 minutes by hand. Allow 1 hour chilling time. Shaping and frying the falafel take about 25 minutes.

**FREEZING**
Cool the fried, drained falafel completely, then open freeze until solid. Transfer to a rigid container, seal, label and freeze for up to 2 months. To serve: fry from frozen.

**BUYING GUIDE**
To save time, buy two 425 g/15 oz cans chick-peas. Drain and rinse, then continue the recipe from the beginning of stage 2.

**SERVING IDEAS**
Serve the falafel with a tangy lemon-flavoured mayonnaise. For a filling lunch, serve the falafel inside a pocket of pitta bread with a salad of sliced tomatoes, cucumber and watercress, and coleslaw and natural yoghurt.

**WATCHPOINT**
Turn the falafel very carefully in the frying-pan, so that they do not break. To make frying easier, first dip in beaten egg, then in flour.

●70 calories/300 kj per falafel

# LEBANON

Every Lebanese restaurant serves chicken cooked with garlic and lemon – it may be pieces of chicken or a poussin, marinated and grilled or cooked in the oven, or kebabs of boned chicken. Grilling, especially over charcoal, is a favourite way of cooking in the Lebanon. In this version, *Jaaj meshwi*, the chicken pieces are coated in spices before grilling, and are served with a cold purée of aubergines, olive oil, lemon juice and garlic.

# Lebanese grilled chicken

SERVES 4

 1.5 kg/3-3½ lb chicken, cut into 8 pieces (see Buying guide)
 juice of 4 large lemons
50 ml/2 fl oz olive oil
2 large cloves garlic, crushed
½ teaspoon salt
pinch of ground allspice
pinch of ground cinnamon
freshly ground black pepper

TO GARNISH
parsley or coriander sprigs
lemon and tomato wedges

1 Place chicken pieces in a large dish.
2 Put the lemon juice, oil, garlic and salt in a blender and work for a few seconds (see Cook's tip).
3 Sprinkle the allspice, cinnamon and pepper over the chicken and rub into the skin.
4 Pour the lemon juice mixture over the chicken and rub in thoroughly. Cover and leave to marinate in a cool place for at least 8 hours or overnight, turning the pieces from time to time.
5 Heat the grill to medium and brush the grill rack with oil.
6 Grill the chicken pieces for about 20-30 minutes, brushing frequently with the marinade, until cooked through (the juices run clear when the thickest part is pierced with a skewer) and the skin is crisp. [!]
7 Transfer the cooked chicken to a warmed serving dish, garnish with parsley or coriander and lemon wedges and tomato. Serve at once with the aubergine purée (see recipe and Serving ideas).

# Aubergine purée

SERVES 4
500 g/1 lb aubergines
3 tablespoons olive oil
about 2 tablespoons lemon juice
1 clove garlic, crushed
salt and freshly ground black pepper

1 Heat the grill to high. Arrange the aubergines in the grill pan and heat under the grill until the skins start to blister and the aubergines are soft to the touch.
2 Put the aubergines in a colander and rinse under cold running water, then peel off the skins (see Steps, right).
3 Squeeze the aubergines over a bowl to remove the bitter juices, then chop the flesh roughly and place in the goblet of a blender (see Cook's tip). Add oil, 2 tablespoons lemon juice and garlic and season to taste with salt and pepper. Work to a smooth purée.
5 Taste the purée and add more lemon juice if liked. Transfer to a serving dish and refrigerate until the purée is required.

## SKINNING AUBERGINES

**1** *Arrange the aubergines on the grill rack and heat until skins blister and the aubergines are soft.*

**2** *Rinse under cold running water, then peel the aubergine skins off in thick strips with a sharp knife.*

## Cook's Notes

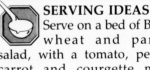

**Lebanese grilled chicken**

**TIME**
Preparation takes about 15 minutes and cooking 20-30 minutes. Allow at least 8 hours for marinating the chicken before cooking.

**BUYING GUIDE**
If preferred, buy 4 large chicken pieces, and cut each piece in half.

**COOK'S TIP**
Blending the marinade emulsifies the mixture, making a creamy sauce which does not separate while the chicken is marinating.

**WATCHPOINT**
When grilling chicken on the bone it is very important to cook it right through to bone. If necessary, cook for longer, on lower heat.

**SERVING IDEAS**
Serve on a bed of Bulgur wheat and parsley salad, with a tomato, pepper, carrot and courgette mixed salad.

● 500 calories/2075 kj per portion

**Aubergine purée**

**TIME**
Total preparation takes about 20 minutes.

**DID YOU KNOW**
This is a version of poor man's caviar – so called because it tastes a little like real caviar, yet costs far less.

**COOK'S TIP**
If you do not have a blender, put aubergine in a bowl and mash with a fork.

● 105 calories/450 kj per portion

# EGYPT

*Ful medames* (pronounced fool maydamez) can be truly regarded as Egypt's national dish. It is eaten by everyone, from the richest to the poorest, and is found on menus in smart restaurants and sold by street vendors. The basic dish is simply cooked beans, but it can be seasoned and flavoured in many different ways – one Cairo restaurant offers 15 varieties of *Ful medames*.

## Ful medames

**SERVES 4-6**
500 g/1 lb dried ful beans, soaked overnight (see Buying guide)
4½ teaspoons ground cumin
4 large cloves garlic, crushed
4 tablespoons olive oil
1.25 L/2 pints water
1 teaspoon sweet paprika
1 teaspoon ground turmeric
salt and freshly ground black pepper

**TO SERVE**
about 150 ml/¼ pint olive oil
3 lemons, cut into wedges
coriander leaves
4 tablespoons chopped fresh parsley
6 hard-boiled eggs (see Variations)

**1** Drain the soaked beans and rinse thoroughly. Put them into a large saucepan and add the cumin, garlic, olive oil and water.
**2** Bring to the boil, then lower the heat, cover and simmer for 1-1½ hours, or until beans are tender and there is just enough juice left in the pan to coat the beans. The water evaporates during the long cooking, leaving a small amount of thick, spicy, gravy-like juice.
**3** Transfer the beans and juice to a large serving bowl, sprinkle over paprika and turmeric and season the mixture with plenty of salt and pepper. Stir well.
**4** To serve: put a small jug of olive oil on a tray or large serving platter. Garnish the lemon with coriander and add to the tray together with the parsley and hard-boiled eggs.
**5** Serve the beans hot or warm and hand the tray of accompaniments separately so that everyone can flavour the beans to taste.

## Cook's Notes

**TIME**
Preparing, cooking and finishing this dish take 1½-2 hours. Allow for overnight soaking of the beans.

**BUYING GUIDE**
Ful beans may be sold as foule medames, dry foul or Nile beans. They are available in packets from Greek delicatessens and Asian shops.

**SERVING IDEAS**
It is traditional for each person to crumble a hard-boiled egg over their beans with a squeeze of lemon juice and olive oil and chopped parsley added to taste.

The beans can also be served with the following selection: Feta cheese, spring onions, watermelon or sweet melon slices, olives, pickled cucumber, a garlic-flavoured tomato sauce and hot pitta bread. Arrange them on a large tray so that everyone can help themselves.

**VARIATIONS**
The hard-boiled eggs can be replaced by the traditional *hamine* eggs or Jewish *Hamindas*, which are baked brown eggs (see Steps).

Add some of the following to the dried ful beans while they are cooking: sliced green or red peppers, tomatoes, chilli sauce and red lentils, for colour as well as flavour.

Canned ful medames are sold in many specialist stores and delicatessens, sometimes called foull medames (Egyptian Nile cooked beans) or foule medames (broad beans). They do not need to be soaked and cooked so are ideal for this recipe if you are in a hurry: simply drain off most of the juice from four 400 g/14 oz cans, then stir in 4 cloves garlic, crushed, 3 tablespoons olive oil, 4½ teaspoons ground cumin. Season with salt and pepper.

●895 calories/3725 kj per portion

**PREPARING HAMINE EGGS**

**1** *Bring eggs to the boil in water with 1 teaspoon oil and ½ teaspoon salt. Gently transfer eggs to an ovenproof dish.*

**2** *Add the cooking water and ½ an unpeeled, sliced onion. Cover and bake in a 110C/225F/Gas ¼ oven for 8-12 hours until dark brown.*

# NORTH AFRICA

Couscous grain is a type of hard-wheat semolina. In Morocco and other North African countries, it is steamed over a rich broth, to make a favourite national dish. The word *couscous* comes from the sound the steam makes as it pushes through the holes of the steamer.

Couscous is ideal for serving a large number of guests as it is best prepared in large quantities, preferably a day in advance. The broth may include any fresh or dry vegetable and any type of meat or fish, flavoured with spices.

## Couscous

**SERVES 10**

1 kg/2 lb stewing lamb, cut in large pieces (see Buying guide)
2 chicken quarters, cut in large pieces (total weight 750 g/1½ lb)
500 g/1 lb stewing beef or veal, cut in large pieces (see Buying guide)
50 g/2 oz chick-peas, soaked in cold water for at least 1 hour
2 large onions, finely chopped
2 cloves garlic, chopped (optional)
½ teaspoon ground ginger
1 teaspoon ground cinnamon
3 whole cloves
freshly ground black pepper
50 g/2 oz seedless raisins or sultanas
6 dried dates, stoned and chopped
2 small turnips, quartered
2 carrots, sliced
½ small white cabbage, shredded
salt
4 courgettes, sliced
100 g/4 oz shelled fresh or frozen broad beans
2 tomatoes, skinned and chopped
6 tablespoons chopped fresh parsley
6 tablespoons chopped fresh coriander (optional, see Did you know)
1.25 kg/3 lb medium, or fine-ground pre-cooked couscous (see Buying guide)
5 tablespoons vegetable oil or 50 g/2 oz butter
1 teaspoon sweet paprika
generous pinch of cayenne or chilli pepper

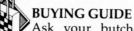
## Cook's Notes

**TIME**
Preparation takes about 1½ hours, including soaking the chick-peas. Cooking takes about 2 hours.

**BUYING GUIDE**
Ask your butcher for any cheap cut of lamb, such as neck. Chuck or skirt are good beef stewing cuts, and the veal often sold in butchers as 'pie veal' would be suitable.
Pre-cooked couscous (steamed, processed and dried) is available in packets in many supermarkets, as well as from Middle Eastern food stores.

**WATCHPOINT**
Do not add any salt until the chick-peas begin to soften, or they will go tough.

**DID YOU KNOW**
Fresh coriander leaves as well as seeds are widely used in Middle Eastern cooking, and can sometimes be obtained from Middle Eastern and Oriental food shops.
In the Middle East, the dish is prepared in a special *couscousier*, a cooking pot with a steamer section on top, not unlike a double boiler.

**PREPARATION**
The usual method for preparing pre-cooked couscous is to place it with a pinch of salt in a bowl, cover with boiling water and leave to soak for about 15 minutes, stirring occasionally, until the liquid is absorbed.

**COOK'S TIPS**
The soaked couscous may just be heated through in a saucepan, but steaming gives a grainier result.

●980 calories/4100 kj per portion

1 Put the lamb, chicken and beef in a very large saucepan (see Did you know). Cover with fresh cold water, bring to the boil and remove the scum with a skimmer or slotted spoon.

2 Drain the chick-peas and add to the pan with the onions, garlic, if using, ginger, cinnamon, cloves and pepper to taste. [!] Cover the pan and simmer for 1 hour.

3 Add the raisins, dates, turnips, carrots, cabbage and salt to taste, and simmer for a further 30 minutes.

4 Add the courgettes, broad beans, tomatoes, parsley and coriander, if using, and simmer for a further 30 minutes.

5 Prepare the pre-cooked couscous according to packet instructions (see Preparation), then mix in the vegetable oil. Place the couscous in a large colander and set it over the vigorously boiling broth in the saucepan (see Cook's tips). When steam begins to rise through the strainer or colander, the couscous is done.

6 To make the sauce: measure out a large cupful of broth, strain and then stir in the sweet paprika and cayenne.

7 To serve: pile the couscous in a pyramid on a warmed round serving platter. Remove the meats and vegetables from the broth with a slotted spoon and arrange them on top of the couscous. Serve the broth in a warmed bowl with a ladle. Hand the hot sauce separately in a jug, for everyone to help themselves.

# KENYA

The tropical island of Lamu lies just above the equator, very close to the northern coast of Kenya in East Africa. Spices grow in abundance there and are widely used to enhance the local food. The islanders live almost exclusively on rice, fish and coconuts, all of which are combined in this very popular dish, called *Samaki wa Lamu* in Swahili.

## Lamu-style fish

SERVES 4-6

1 kg/2 lb haddock fillets, defrosted if frozen, skinned and cut into 5 × 2.5 cm/2 × 1 inch pieces (see Did you know)
4 cloves garlic, crushed
juice of 2 limes
1½ teaspoons ground cumin
1 teaspoon salt
1 teaspoon freshly ground black pepper
3 tablespoons sunflower oil
lime slices, to garnish

1 In a small bowl, mix the garlic and lime juice to a paste with the cumin, salt and pepper. Spread the mixture over the fish. Set aside on a plate while cooking the rice (see recipe).

2 When rice is cooked heat oil in a large frying-pan, add fish and fry over moderate heat for 8 minutes, turning carefully with a fish slice halfway through. ⚠ Drain on absorbent paper.

3 Arrange the fried fish on a warmed serving dish, garnish with lime slices and serve at once.

## Coconut rice

SERVES 4-6

250 g/9 oz long-grain rice, washed and drained
100 g/4 oz creamed coconut, cut into small pieces (see Buying guide) or 175 g/6 oz desiccated coconut
300 ml/½ pint hot water
3 tablespoons sunflower oil
1 tablespoon salt

1 Put the creamed coconut pieces into a bowl, pour over the hot water and stir until the coconut has dissolved. If using desiccated coconut, pour over 850 ml/1½ pints boiling water (the coconut will retain some water), leave to infuse for 20 minutes. Strain, pressing coconut with back of spoon to extract as much liquid as possible.

2 Heat the oil in a heavy-based saucepan, add the drained rice and stir until each grain is coated with oil. Pour in the coconut liquid to just cover, topping up with a little boiling water if necessary. Add the salt, stir well and bring to the boil. Cover the pan, turn down the heat as low as possible and simmer for 12-15 minutes or until the rice is tender and all the liquid has been completely absorbed.

3 Remove the coconut rice from the heat and keep in a warm place until ready to serve.

---

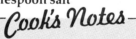

## Cook's Notes

**Lamu-style fish**

**TIME**
Preparation 10 minutes, cooking about 8 minutes.

**WATCHPOINT**
Take care not to over-brown the fish; it is meant to be lightly coloured.

**DID YOU KNOW**
In Lamu, the firm-fleshed kingfish would most likely be used. Haddock makes an excellent substitute.

**SERVING IDEAS**
Lightly cooked spinach mixed with fried onion and tomato and flavoured with mild curry powder makes a delicious accompaniment to the fried fish and coconut rice. In Lamu, the fish, rice and accompanying vegetables would be served on separate brass platters. You may, however, prefer to arrange the fish on a large serving dish with the rice in a ring around it.

This dish is served for the evening meal locally. It would be followed by sticky, fudge-like sweetmeats and Turkish-style coffee flavoured with cardamom or ginger. Because Lamu has been visited by Arab spice traders since the Middle Ages, the island's culture, reflected in its food, is a fascinating blend of Arab and African characteristics.

●255 calories/1050 kj per portion

**Coconut rice**

**TIME**
Preparation takes about 5 minutes, cooking about 15 minutes.

**BUYING GUIDE**
Creamed coconut is the shredded flesh of the coconut, drained of liquid and pressed into a solid block. It is widely used in Asian cooking and is available from Asian food shops and large supermarkets.

**DID YOU KNOW**
A cone made of plaited grass—a *kawa* (see photograph)—is used to cover food before serving.

●510 calories/2150 kj per portion

# CANADA

Each spring in the maple woods of Canada the sap begins to rise in the trees, and the clear fluid is transformed in sugaring cabins to rich, amber-coloured maple syrup. Canada also produces very fine bacon and in this recipe for Maple ham the two make a delicious, uniquely Canadian combination. Serve the baked, clove-flavoured gammon joint with traditional cornbread muffins, made with cornmeal, which the Canadians call Johnny cakes.

## Maple ham

SERVES 6-8

2 kg/4½-5 lb corner or middle
    gammon joint, boned
15-20 cloves

TO GLAZE
125 ml/4 fl oz maple syrup
3 tablespoons light soft brown
    sugar
1 teaspoon mustard powder

1 Cover the gammon with cold water and leave to soak for 3-4 hours.
2 Heat the oven to 190C/375F/Gas 5.
3 Dry the gammon with absorbent paper. Using a sharp knife and kitchen scissors, if necessary, remove the skin and some of the fat below it. Using a sharp knife, score the fat surface of the joint in a trellis pattern, cutting about 5 mm/¼ inch deep. Stud the intersections with cloves (see Steps).
4 Weigh the gammon and calculate the cooking time at 35 minutes per 500 g/1 lb. Put the gammon in a roasting tin and roast in the oven for the calculated cooking time.
5 Meanwhile, make the glaze: combine the maple syrup, sugar and mustard powder in a bowl and stir well to mix.
6 Forty-five minutes before the end of the calculated cooking time, remove the gammon from the oven and spoon half the glaze over the scored surface. Return to the oven for 15 minutes, then spoon over the remaining glaze and roast for the remaining 30 minutes, until golden brown. Transfer to a warmed serving platter and serve hot.

## Cook's Notes

**TIME**
Preparation takes about 25 minutes, roasting in the oven about 2½-3 hours. Soak at least 3-4 hours.

**COOK'S TIP**
Use any left-over maple syrup on waffles, pancakes or ice-cream.

●675 calories/2825 kj per portion

### HOW TO TRELLIS GAMMON

**1** *Score the fat surface in a trellis pattern with a sharp knife.*

**2** *Stud the centres of the trellis with cloves.*

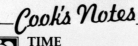

Raisin soured cream pie is a typical example of the Canadian way of mixing together unusual ingredients. With a rich sweet pastry that tastes equally good hot or cold, this pie can be served as an alternative to mince pies at Christmas or pumpkin pie on Thanksgiving Day.

# Raisin soured cream pie

**MAKES 6-8 SLICES**
275 g/10 oz plain flour
2 teaspoons baking powder
pinch of salt
75 g/3 oz caster sugar
¼ teaspoon vanilla flavouring
1 egg, separated
1 tablespoon milk
150 g/5 oz butter or margarine, diced
milk, for brushing

**FILLING**
225 g/8 oz seedless raisins
150 ml/¼ pint soured cream
1 teaspoon ground cinnamon
¼ teaspoon ground cloves
¼ teaspoon freshly grated nutmeg
2 eggs
50 g/2 oz dark soft brown sugar
50 g/2 oz pecan nuts, chopped (see Buying guide)

1 Heat the oven to 200C/400F/Gas 6.
2 Make the filling: put the raisins into a large bowl and stir in the soured cream and spices. Mix well, then set aside while making pastry.
3 Sift the flour, baking powder and salt into a bowl. Make a well in the centre and add the sugar, vanilla flavouring, half the egg yolk and all the egg white and the milk. Stir until well mixed together.
4 Beat the butter into the mixture, then knead lightly to form a smooth dough. Wrap in cling film and refrigerate for 30 minutes.
5 Roll out half the pastry on a lightly floured surface and use to line a 23 cm/9 inch flan tin.
6 Beat the eggs in a small bowl, then stir into the soured cream and fruit mixture. Stir in the brown sugar and nuts and mix well.
7 Pour the filling into the pastry

## Cook's Notes

**TIME**
Preparation, including chilling the pastry, takes 1 hour. Cooking takes 30 minutes, plus 15 minutes cooling.

**SERVING IDEAS**
Serve the raisin pie warm with a jug of thick cream for a special dessert, or leave until cold, slice and serve with coffee.

**BUYING GUIDE**
Pecan nuts are available ready-packaged in health food shops and some delicatessens. They come from America where they are used to make pecan pie. They are quite expensive, but have a unique flavour and texture, much loved by North Americans. Walnuts can be used instead, if liked, for a more economical dessert.

**FREEZING**
Leave pie until cold, then wrap in a polythene bag, seal, label and freeze for up to 2 months. To serve: defrost for 3-4 hours, then cover the pie in foil and warm in a 180C/350F/Gas 4 oven for about 20-25 minutes.

●655 calories/2750 kj per slice

case and smooth top with a knife. Roll out remaining pastry and use to make a lid. Prick top with a fork, then mix the remaining egg yolk with a little milk and brush the top of the pastry.
8 Bake in the oven for 30 minutes or until the pastry is golden brown. Remove from the oven and leave to cool for 15 minutes. Remove from tin  and serve warm or cold.

# UNITED STATES

Maryland, one of the south-eastern states of America, is well known for the fine quality of the chickens raised there, and has given its name to a justly famous fried chicken dish. There are many variations of the true Chicken Maryland, some of which have been passed down from mother to daughter in hand-written family cookery books. But the real thing is always served with a cream gravy and 'corn oysters'—delicate sweetcorn fritters.

This version of the recipe comes from an old Baltimore family: its 'two-coat' method of creating a deliciously crispy crust is said to have been devised by a family cook long before the Civil War.

The 'Chicken Maryland' with fried bananas and bacon that is so popular in many other countries is very tasty in its own way but it bears little resemblance to the genuine article and is unknown in the United States.

# Chicken Maryland

**SERVES 6**

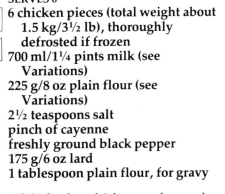

**6 chicken pieces (total weight about 1.5 kg/3½ lb), thoroughly defrosted if frozen**
**700 ml/1¼ pints milk (see Variations)**
**225 g/8 oz plain flour (see Variations)**
**2½ teaspoons salt**
**pinch of cayenne**
**freshly ground black pepper**
**175 g/6 oz lard**
**1 tablespoon plain flour, for gravy**

1 Wash the chicken and pat dry with absorbent paper. Arrange in a single layer in a large roasting tin and pour over 300 ml/½ pint of the milk. Cover with cling film and refrigerate for about 30 minutes.
2 Remove the chicken pieces, and set the tin of milk aside. Put the 225 g/8 oz flour in a polythene bag with the salt, cayenne and pepper to taste. Shake well to mix, then add the chicken pieces one or two at a time. Shake the bag vigorously until the chicken is well coated in the seasoned flour.
3 When all the pieces have been floured, dip them in the reserved milk in the roasting tin, then toss them again in the bag of seasoned flour.
4 Heat oven to 110C/225F/Gas ¼.
5 In a large, heavy frying-pan melt enough lard to come to a depth of about 4 cm/1½ inches. Heat until very hot, then lower the heat and fry the chicken pieces, [!] skin side down, until brown on one side, then turn them carefully and fry until brown on the other side.

## Cook's Notes

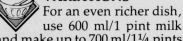

**TIME**
Preparation takes 40 minutes, including chilling the chicken pieces. Cooking the chicken takes just under 1 hour, and making the gravy about 8 minutes.

**VARIATIONS**
For an even richer dish, use 600 ml/1 pint milk and make up to 700 ml/1¼ pints with single cream
Plain white flour is traditional for this recipe, but wholemeal flour gives a nuttier coating.

**WATCHPOINT**
The chicken must be fried slowly and turned frequently so that the crust is not broken.

**SERVING IDEAS**
Mashed potatoes or rice go very well with Chicken Maryland, since they absorb the cream gravy well.

●355 calories/1475 kj per portion

Continue to cook over low-to-moderate heat, turning the pieces frequently, for about 30 minutes or until the chicken is thoroughly cooked (the juices should run clear when the thickest part is pierced with a fine skewer).
6 Remove the chicken pieces, drain quickly on absorbent paper, then arrange on a warmed serving platter. Keep hot in the oven while making the gravy and corn oysters.
7 Make the cream gravy: pour the fat from the frying-pan into a heat-proof bowl. Measure out 2 table-spoons, and pour this amount back into the pan. Stir in 1 tablespoon flour and cook, stirring, for about 1 minute, then gradually stir in the remaining 425 ml/¾ pint milk.
8 Bring slowly to the boil, stirring constantly, then lower the heat and simmer until the gravy is thick, scraping up the sediment from the base and sides of the pan. Pour the gravy into a warmed gravy boat and keep hot in the oven with the chicken while cooking the corn oysters.

# Corn oysters

**SERVES 6**

**75 g/3 oz plain flour**
**½ teaspoon baking powder**
**generous pinch of salt**
**300 g/10½ oz can cream-style sweetcorn**
**2 eggs**
**bacon dripping or lard, for frying**

1 Sift the flour, baking powder and salt together on to a plate. Put the sweetcorn in a bowl.
2 Whisk the eggs until light and fluffy. Add them to the sweetcorn and mix well. Fold in the flour mixture until no trace of flour is visible in the batter.
3 Generously grease a heavy frying-pan or girdle with bacon dripping, and heat until a drop of water flicked over the surface splutters. Cook the corn oysters in batches, dropping heaped teaspoonfuls of the sweet-corn mixture into the pan, about 2.5 cm/1 inch apart. Cook over high heat until the 'oysters' are browned underneath. Turn them with a palette knife or fish slice and cook on the other side until brown.
4 When the 'oysters' are ready transfer them to a baking sheet lined with absorbent paper and keep warm in the oven with the chicken until all are cooked. Serve as soon as they are all ready, arranged around the fried chicken on a serving platter or on a separate dish.

## Cook's Notes

**TIME**
Preparing the sweetcorn mixture takes 3-4 minutes, and frying the corn oysters about 15 minutes.

**DID YOU KNOW**
Corn oysters are so called because they are oyster-shaped and taste rather like batter-fried oysters, which are another speciality of Maryland and other coastal regions of the United States.

●130 calories/525 kj per portion

Gumbo – an African word for okra – became the name of a hearty soup traditional to Louisiana when okra was brought to the American Deep South by the African slave ships in the 18th century. Okra, a tapering green vegetable which is actually the seed pod of a type of hibiscus, is a main ingredient of this delicious soup, which is poured over freshly cooked rice to serve. Gumbo may be made with a variety of seafood, but this prawn version is the most popular, since prawns are so plentiful along the Louisiana coast.

# Prawn gumbo

SERVES 4
500 g/1 lb okra, thinly sliced (see Buying guide)
500 g/1 lb peeled prawns, defrosted if frozen
50 g/2 oz butter
1 onion, finely chopped
1 green pepper, deseeded and finely chopped
1 clove garlic, crushed
2 tablespoons plain flour
1 L/1¾ pints chicken stock
250 g/9 oz tomatoes, skinned and chopped
bouquet garni (2 sprigs parsley, 1 sprig thyme, 1 bay leaf)
good pinch of cayenne
salt and freshly ground black pepper

1 Melt the butter in a large saucepan, add the onion, green pepper and garlic and fry gently for 5 minutes until the onion is soft and lightly coloured. Sprinkle in the flour and cook for a further 2 minutes, stirring constantly with a wooden spoon.
2 Pour in the chicken stock, stir well and bring to the boil. Add the okra, tomatoes, bouquet garni and cayenne, and season to taste with salt and pepper. Lower the heat, cover the pan and simmer very gently for 30 minutes, until the okra is very tender.
3 Remove and discard the bouquet garni. Add the prawns and cook gently for a further 2-3 minutes, stirring once or twice, until they are heated through.
4 Serve the gumbo in warmed deep soup bowls over Lemon rice (see recipe on next page).

# Lemon rice

SERVES 4
225 g/8 oz long-grain rice
25 g/1 oz butter
1 tablespoon lemon juice
½ teaspoon salt and a little freshly
    ground black pepper
350 ml/12 fl oz water

1 Rinse the rice several times under cold running water, then drain.
2 Put the rice, butter, lemon juice, salt and pepper in a large saucepan. Pour in the water. Bring quickly to the boil. Stir once, then cover and cook over very gentle heat for about 20 minutes until all the liquid is absorbed and the rice is tender.
3 Leave the rice to stand, covered, for about 10 minutes, then spoon a portion into each of 4 soup bowls and pour over the prawn gumbo.

## Cook's Notes

**Prawn gumbo**

**TIME**
Preparation takes about 10 minutes, cooking about 40 minutes.

**BUYING GUIDE**
Okra is available from Asian, Greek and West Indian food shops as well as street markets and some large supermarkets.
Okra is also available canned, but would not be suitable for this dish, in which the flavour and texture of fresh okra are essential. Canned okra is best used in casseroled dishes.

**SERVING IDEAS**
The prawn gumbo should be served as a main course, accompanied by chunks of French bread and a green salad. Serve a full-bodied dry white wine such as Mâcon with it, and complete the meal with a fresh-tasting dessert: sliced mango or pineapple for example, or a lemon sorbet.

**DID YOU KNOW**
Okra — sometimes known as 'ladies' fingers' because of the tapering shape of its pods — is very popular in Asian and African cooking. It has a special affinity with lamb and tomatoes. In the original Creole recipes for gumbo, a delicious green vegetable stock called *z'herbes* (Creole for French *les herbes*) was often used: it was made from spinach, beet tops, watercress, lettuce and parsley. If you have time, make a well-seasoned stock from these vegetables and use it instead of chicken stock for a beautiful colour.

●290 calories/1225 kj per portion

**Lemon rice**
**TIME**
Cooking the rice takes about 20 minutes. Allow 10 minutes standing.

●250 calories/1050 kj per portion

Texas produces some of the world's finest beef, so it is not surprising that spicy Chilli con carne (*con carne* means 'with meat') is enormously popular there. This Texan chilli is adapted from the Mexican version, which originally used beef introduced to the New World by Spain.

Chilli con carne traditionally consists of cubed or minced beef and dried red chillies (hot chilli powder gives excellent results in place of dried chillies). In Mexico it is sometimes thickened with *masa harina*, the cornmeal used to make Mexican *tortillas* or pancakes. Onions, tomatoes and garlic may also be included in the chilli; cooked red kidney beans can be added just before the end of cooking time, or served separately.

Easy to prepare and very tasty, Chilli con carne (see Did you know) is perfect for a family meal or informal party; just adjust the quantities according to the number you have to feed.

# Chilli con carne

**SERVES 4**

250 g/9 oz dried red kidney beans
   (see Buying guide)
3 onions, finely chopped
1 bay leaf
3 tablespoons vegetable oil
500 g/1 lb lean beef, minced
   (see Buying guide)
1 clove garlic, crushed
2 teaspoons dried oregano
1 teaspoon ground cumin
1 teaspoon chilli powder
1 tablespoon sweet paprika
freshly ground black pepper
400 g/14 oz can tomatoes, roughly
   chopped, with their juice
300 ml/½ pint beef stock
salt

**1** Wash and pick over the beans, then place in a large bowl and cover with cold water. Leave to soak for 8 hours, preferably overnight.
**2** Drain the soaked beans, rinse thoroughly under cold running water, then put them into a large saucepan with one-third of the chopped onions and the bay leaf.

Pour in fresh cold water to cover and bring to the boil. Boil fast for 10 minutes. [!] Reduce the heat to low, cover the pan, and leave the beans to simmer for 1½-2 hours. During cooking check the pan from time to time and add extra boiling water as needed.

3 Start to cook the meat when the beans have been cooking for about 30 minutes: heat the oil in a large, heavy frying-pan. Add the beef, the remaining onions and the garlic, and cook until the beef is lightly browned, breaking it up with a wooden spoon.

4 Transfer the beef mixture to a 2 L/3½ pint flameproof casserole. Add the oregano, cumin, chilli powder, sweet paprika and black pepper to taste. Stir well to mix. Add the tomatoes with their juice and the beef stock. Simmer, partially covered, for 1-1½ hours until the beef is tender.

5 About 15 minutes before the meat is ready, test the beans; by now they should be almost tender. Add 2 teaspoons salt to the pan. Continue to boil until the beans are tender, without adding more water. [!] Sieve and drain thoroughly.

6 Add the beans to the meat mixture in the casserole and continue to simmer for 10-15 minutes, until heated through. Serve at once straight from the dish.

## Cook's Notes

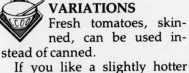

**TIME**
Preparation and cooking take about 2½ hours. Remember to soak the beans for 8 hours or overnight.

**VARIATIONS**
Fresh tomatoes, skinned, can be used instead of canned.

If you like a slightly hotter chilli, add more chilli powder to taste.

**SERVING IDEAS**
Serve with boiled rice and a green salad. Cold beer or lager, or iced lime juice would be refreshing to drink with this hot dish.

**FREEZING**
Cool quickly, then pack in a polythene bag or rigid container. Seal, label and freeze for up to 2 months. To serve: defrost from frozen in a heavy-based saucepan until bubbling, stirring constantly and adding a little water if the mixture seems dry.

**BUYING GUIDE**
Take care to buy pulses from a store with a quick turnover; stale pulses will never become tender however long they are soaked and cooked. Even pre-packaged pulses need to be washed, to remove any dirt or grit remaining.

Instead of buying minced beef from the supermarket or butcher, buy good-quality chuck steak and mince it

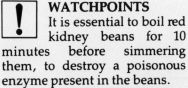

yourself—the end result will taste infinitely better; ready-prepared minced beef can be very fatty.

**COOK'S TIP**
Chilli con carne can be made the day before and refrigerated overnight. Let it come to room temperature for about 2 hours before reheating until bubbling.

**WATCHPOINTS**
It is essential to boil red kidney beans for 10 minutes before simmering them, to destroy a poisonous enzyme present in the beans.

Do not add any more water after salting the beans, as the cooked beans should be quite dry. If necessary, finish off the cooking with the pan uncovered, to make any surplus liquid evaporate more quickly.

**DID YOU KNOW**
Chilli is the English spelling for the Spanish and Mexican word *chili*, meaning hot red peppers. Although the full title of the dish is *chilli con carne*, it is usually only referred to as *chilli*.

The long cooking time is intentional because of the chilli powder in the recipe. If only cooked for a short time, the finished dish will taste raw and the flavour of the chilli will not have time to mature and be absorbed into the meat.

●520 calories/2175 kj per portion

Pecan pie originated in the American Deep South, where the early settlers in the seventeenth century found pecan nut trees growing in Georgia. Nowadays there are almost as many 'classic' pecan pie recipes as there are American states. One famous Georgian cook of the 1920s, Mrs James Sutcliffe, insisted on including molasses to make her pie filling even richer.

Because of the richness of the filling, most people prefer pecan pie made with plain shortcrust pastry, as in our recipe. But some New Orleans cooks make it with *pâte brisée* (shortcrust enriched with egg yolk), reflecting their French heritage. Some recipes use an unbaked pastry shell, so that the filling seeps right through the crust during cooking. Our version, from Georgia, is made with a pie crust baked blind, to give the base a slightly crunchy texture.

# Pecan pie

SERVES 8

215 g/7½ oz shortcrust pastry, defrosted if frozen

FILLING

175 g/6 oz light soft brown sugar
250 g/9 oz golden syrup
75 g/3 oz butter (see Cook's tip)
½ teaspoon salt
3 large eggs
150 g/5 oz pecan halves (see Buying guide)
1 teaspoon vanilla flavouring

1 Heat the oven to 230C/450F/Gas 8.
2 Roll out the pastry thinly on a lightly floured surface and use it to line a 23 cm/9 inch pie plate. Reserve the trimmings. Brush the edges of the pastry with a little water.
3 Roll out trimmings to a 20 × 5 cm/8 × 2 inch rectangle. Cut into 3 strips. Twist strips at regular intervals (see Step 1) and brush 1 side with a little water. Press the moistened sides around edge of plate (see Step 2) and press to seal joins.
4 Prick the pastry base in several places with a fork. Place a circle of greaseproof paper or foil in the pastry case: weight it down with a thick, even layer of baking beans. Bake blind for 8-10 minutes.
5 Meanwhile, put the sugar, syrup, butter and salt in a small heavy-based saucepan and heat gently until the sugar is completely dissolved. Remove from the heat.
6 Remove the pastry case from the oven, remove the foil and beans and leave the pastry case to cool. Lower oven to 180C/350F/Gas 4.
7 Beat the eggs well in a bowl, then

## Cook's Notes

**TIME**
Preparing the pastry case, baking blind and making the filling takes about 40 minutes. Baking in the oven takes about 50 minutes. Allow 30 minutes cooling time, then 1 hour chilling.

**SERVING IDEAS**
Always serve pecan pie cold, cut into small wedges as it is very rich and filling. Unsweetened whipped cream makes a very good accompaniment.
    Pecan pie makes an excellent addition to a picnic: pack it in the pie plate in which it was baked.

**WATCHPOINT**
If the edge browns too fast as the pie bakes, cover it with a strip of foil to prevent it burning.

**COOK'S TIP**
Butter is an essential ingredient in the pie filling. Do not be tempted to use margarine instead as this will be a false economy: the pie will not have the right flavour.

**STORAGE**
Pecan pie keeps well. Covered with cling film, it can be stored in the refrigerator for up to 1 week.

**BUYING GUIDE**
Pecan nuts are similar in appearance to walnuts, to which they are related, but are longer with a more oval shape, and have a sweeter taste. They should be a glossy deep brown and firm and slightly brittle, not limp or dull-looking. They are available ready-packaged in health food shops and some delicatessens. Walnuts may be used instead.
    It is worth buying more pecan nuts than you need for this recipe—they will be cheaper this way. Store those you do not use in an airtight container and use them to make biscuits.

●500 calories/2075 kj per slice

**MAKING THE TRIMMING**

1 *Twisting the pastry strips for the edge of the pie.*

2 *Press the twisted pastry strips round the edge of the pie plate.*

gradually stir in the melted syrup mixture. Reserve eight of the best pecan halves. Coarsely chop the remainder and stir into the filling mixture. Stir in the vanilla flavouring and beat well.
8 Pour the filling mixture evenly into the prepared pastry case and carefully arrange the reserved pecan halves in a circle round the edge.
9 Bake the pie in the oven for about 50 minutes, until the centre of the filling is beginning to set. Cool, cover with cling film and refrigerate for at least 1 hour. Serve cold (see Serving ideas).

# MEXICO

Avocados were cultivated in Mexico as far back as 7000 B.C. and *guacamole*, made from mashed avocados with spicy flavourings, is an ancient Mexican dish which remains as popular today as it has ever been. It can be served in a variety of ways, but is most often eaten as a dip.

## Guacamole

SERVES 4

2 ripe avocados (see Buying guide)

100 g/4 oz tomatoes, skinned, deseeded and finely chopped

1 tablespoon finely chopped onion (see Cook's tips)

1 teaspoon hot green chilli pepper, deseeded and finely chopped (see Variations)

1 tablespoon finely chopped fresh coriander leaves or flat-leaved parsley

salt

lemon slice and parsley, to garnish

1 Cut the avocados in half and remove the stones. Scoop out the avocado flesh with a spoon and put it in a large bowl. Mash the avocado flesh well with a fork until it is smooth and creamy.

2 Add all the other ingredients and mix very thoroughly to blend (see Cook's tips).

3 Transfer the guacamole mixture to a serving bowl. Fork it up and garnish with a lemon twist and parsley sprigs. Serve the guacamole at once (see Cook's tips).

# Cook's Notes

**TIME**
Preparation takes only 10 minutes.

**COOK'S TIPS**
Do not exceed this amount of chopped onion or the flavour of the avocado will be lost.

Although the ingredients are finely chopped, the guacamole should have a slightly chunky texture, with a definite 'bite' to it. So, combine the ingredients by hand, not in a food processor, or the mixture will be too smooth.

As avocado discolours easily, guacamole should be served as soon as it is ready. Otherwise, cover the bowl with cling film and chill in the refrigerator until required: just before serving, turn the surface over with a fork if it has discoloured slightly.

There is a theory that placing the avocado stone in a dish containing an avocado mixture prevents it from discolouring. Although many people swear by it, there is no actual scientific proof that it works!

**BUYING GUIDE**
To test for ripeness, press the thin end of the avocado gently: it is ripe if the flesh 'gives' slightly. To avoid bruised avocados, buy them when underripe and leave them on a sunny windowsill for a few days to ripen slowly.

**DID YOU KNOW**
Guacamole gets its name from *aguacate*, the Mexican word for avocado.

**VARIATIONS**
A dash of Tabasco may replace the chopped chilli pepper.

**SERVING IDEAS**
In Mexico, guacamole is usually served with fried wedges of *tortilla*, a type of pancake in which a special flour called *masa harina*, made from boiled maize, is used.

Potato crisps or sliced pitta bread would be excellent for scooping up the guacamole, or it can be served with a selection of crudités as an appetizer with drinks.

Try guacamole as a starter or side salad, served in individual bowls lined with lettuce leaves. Alternatively, scoop out raw large tomatoes and fill them with guacamole to make an unusual vegetable accompaniment.

Guacamole also makes a delicious sauce with poached or baked white fish or cold meat such as chicken, turkey or pork.

●165 calories/700 kj per portion

# BRAZIL

This rich chocolate mousse, with its deliciously different flavour, is very popular with the Brazilians who love sweet dishes, and it combines two ingredients native to South America: chocolate and cashew nuts. Chocolate, which originated in Mexico, was drunk by the ancient Aztecs before it was discovered by the Spaniards in the 16th century, while cashew nuts, which grow profusely and are used extensively in Brazil, are even included in the making of an alcoholic drink called *cajuada*.

## Mousse de castanhas de caju e chocolate

SERVES 6-8

50 g/2 oz plain dark chocolate, broken into small pieces (see Buying guide)
3 tablespoons hot water
100 g/4 oz caster sugar
5 eggs, separated
100 g/4 oz cashew nuts, finely ground (see Buying guide and Preparation)
300 ml/½ pint double cream
pinch of salt
few whole cashew nuts, to decorate

1 Put the chocolate in the top of a double boiler or a bowl set over a saucepan of simmering water. Add the water and sugar and stir with a wooden spoon over low heat until the chocolate is completely melted and the sugar fully dissolved (see Steps).

2 Remove from the heat. Remove the top section of the double boiler or the bowl from the hot water. Using a balloon whisk, beat in the egg yolks one at a time, beating well after each addition until they are fully incorporated. Set the chocolate and egg mixture aside to cool for about 15 minutes.

3 Lightly stir the ground cashew nuts into the cooled chocolate and egg mixture.

4 Put 225 ml/8 fl oz of the cream and the egg whites in separate clean dry bowls. Whip the cream until standing in soft peaks. Whisk the egg whites until standing in stiff peaks. Using a large metal spoon, lightly fold first the cream, then the whisked egg whites into the chocolate mixture.

5 Pour the mixture into a glass serving bowl, cover with cling film and refrigerate overnight or until the mousse is set.

6 Just before serving, whip the remaining cream until standing in soft peaks. Pipe rosettes of cream around the edge of the mousse and top each rosette with a cashew nut. Serve the chocolate and cashew nut mousse chilled.

## Cook's Notes

**TIME**
Preparation takes about 25 minutes, then allow for overnight chilling. Finishing the chocolate mousse takes about 5 minutes.

**COOK'S TIP**
This is a perfect dessert to serve at a dinner party: as it needs to be made the day before to ensure that it sets and that the flavours develop, there is only the decoration to do on the night of the party.

**PREPARATION**
Grind the nuts in a blender, food processor or coffee grinder. They must be finely ground, but avoid over-grinding, or they will be reduced to a paste.

●495 calories/2075 kj per portion

**BUYING GUIDE**
French semi-sweet chocolate is ideal for this recipe. Ordinary plain dessert chocolate may be used but, in this case, cut down slightly on the sugar.

Cashew nuts are roasted before they are edible, as the nut shell contains a toxic oil which must be removed by the roasting process. Shelled cashews are available plain or salted: use plain nuts for this recipe.

**SERVING IDEAS**
Serve the mousse with crisp *langues de chat* biscuits or sponge fingers, if liked.

Follow the rich mousse with small cups of strong, piping hot black coffee and a glass of Tia Maria liqueur for a special occasion: the coffee flavour complements chocolate perfectly.

**TWO WAYS TO MELT CHOCOLATE**

1 Melt the broken-up chocolate in a flameproof bowl set over a pan of simmering water.

2 Melt the chocolate in the top of a double boiler.

# USSR

This sumptuously rich dish was the brainchild of a 19th century French chef, who was faced with the hazards of a Siberian winter and the demands of his gourmet Russian patron, Count Stroganoff. Frustrated in his attempts to cope with permanently frozen beef, the chef decided to cut it into tiny, thin strips, then fry it and serve it in a soured cream and mushroom sauce. The result seems to have found favour with the Count.

## Beef Stroganoff

SERVES 4
500 g/1 lb fillet steak, trimmed of fat (see Buying guide)
freshly ground black pepper
2 tablespoons vegetable oil
50 g/2 oz butter
1 onion, thinly sliced
250 g/9 oz small button mushrooms, thinly sliced
300 ml/½ pint soured cream (see Buying guide)
2-3 teaspoons French mustard, according to taste
salt
chopped fresh parsley, to garnish

1 Lay the meat flat and beat it well with a wooden rolling pin. Cut it into 5 mm/¼ inch thick slices. Cut each slice across the grain into 5 mm/¼ inch wide strips, 2.5-5 cm/1-2 inches long (see Steps). Sprinkle with pepper and set aside.
2 Heat half the oil and butter in a wide shallow pan, add the onion and fry over low heat for 10 minutes until soft and golden, stirring frequently.
3 Increase the heat a little, add the mushrooms and fry for a further 2 minutes, stirring constantly. Cover the pan, remove from the heat and set aside.
4 Heat the remaining oil and butter in a separate, large shallow frying-pan. When sizzling hot, add half the beef strips and fry over high heat [!] for about 1 minute, turning constantly until the beef is sealed.
5 Remove the meat from the pan with a slotted spoon and keep hot in the covered pan with the onion and mushrooms. Fry the remaining meat in the same way.

6 Stir the soured cream and mustard into the beef and vegetables, add salt and pepper to taste, then place over gentle heat and bring to just below boiling point, stirring constantly.

7 Spoon the Beef Stroganoff on to warmed individual dishes. Garnish the top of each portion with a sprinkling of chopped fresh parsley and serve the Stroganoff at once, piping hot (see Serving ideas).

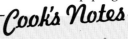Cook's Notes

**TIME**
Allow about 20 minutes for preparing the meat and vegetables and another 20 minutes for cooking.

**BUYING GUIDE**
All parts of a fillet of beef are very tender; the pointed rib end is usually less expensive than the thick centre cuts, and is perfectly suitable for this dish.
If soured cream is unavailable, simply stir 2 teaspoons lemon juice into 300 ml/½ pint fresh double cream.

● 445 calories/1850 kj per portion

**VARIATIONS**
Thinly sliced fillet (tenderloin) of pork, or veal or lamb kidneys, can be used to make a delicious pork or kidney Stroganoff.

**SERVING IDEAS**
Because it is a rich dish, only a plain accompaniment is needed: spoon on to a bed of boiled rice or noodles. Serve a green salad separately.

**WATCHPOINT**
The strips of beef must be fried rapidly to seal in the juices and keep the meat succulent.

### PREPARING STRIPS OF BEEF

1 With a sharp knife, cut the beef lengthways into slices 5 mm/¼ inch thick.

2 Cut each slice across the grain of the meat into 5 mm/¼ inch wide strips, 2.5-5 cm/1-2 inches long.

Chicken Kiev was created in and named after the beautiful capital city of the Ukraine, in the south-west of the USSR. In this internationally renowned dish, the chicken breasts are stuffed with garlic butter, then deep-fried until the crumb coating is golden and crisp, and the meat inside tender and succulent.

# Chicken Kiev

**SERVES 4**

4 chicken breast and wing pieces, skinned, each weighing about 250 g/9 oz (see Buying guide)
100 g/4 oz unsalted butter, softened
¼ teaspoon finely grated lemon zest
2 teaspoons lemon juice
1-2 cloves garlic, finely crushed
1 tablespoon finely chopped fresh parsley
salt and freshly ground black pepper
2 tablespoons plain flour
100 g/4 oz fine dry white breadcrumbs
2 eggs
vegetable oil, for deep frying
cutlet frills, to finish
parsley sprigs and lemon wedges, to garnish

1 Put the butter, lemon zest and juice, garlic and parsley in a small bowl, with salt and pepper to taste. Beat with a wooden spoon until smoothly blended.
2 Transfer to a flat plate and shape into a rectangle 6 cm/2½ inches long. Cover butter and refrigerate for at least 4 hours until firm. []
3 Prepare the chicken breasts: with a small sharp knife, remove any breastbone and cut away the wing tips just below the first joint.
4 Lay the chicken breasts on a board or work surface, skinned side down and with the thickest part towards you. Make a pocket in each breast by slitting the breast horizontally, taking care not to pierce the flesh at either end or on the far side (see Step 1).
5 Cut the block of butter lengthways into 4 equal fingers. Insert into the pockets (see Step 2) and

then close the pockets (see Step 3).
6 Spread the flour and breadcrumbs out on separate flat plates and season the flour well with salt and pepper. Beat the eggs in a shallow dish.
7 Dip each stuffed chicken breast first in flour, to coat thoroughly all over, tapping off the excess. Then dip in beaten egg and finally in breadcrumbs, to coat thoroughly. Press the coating on firmly with a palette knife. Dip the coated breasts again in egg, then in breadcrumbs. Press the coating on again, transfer to a plate, cover and refrigerate for 1-2 hours, to firm the coating.
8 Heat the oven to 110C/225F/Gas ¼.

9 Pour enough oil into a deep-fat frier to come halfway up the sides. Heat to 180C/350F or until a stale bread cube browns in 60 seconds. [] Lower 2 of the chicken breasts into the hot oil and fry for 12-15 minutes, turning once, until golden and cooked through.
10 Remove the cooked chicken breasts from the oil, drain on absorbent paper and keep hot in the oven while frying the remaining chicken breasts in the same way.
11 Slip a cutlet frill on to each wing joint. Arrange the chicken breasts on a warmed serving dish, garnish with parsley sprigs and lemon wedges and serve at once. []

## Cook's Notes

**TIME**
Allow 4 hours chilling time for the butter. Preparing the chicken breasts takes about 30 minutes, then allow a further 1-2 hours chilling time. Frying takes about 30 minutes.

**BUYING GUIDE**
Large, thick, firm chicken breasts are required for Chicken Kiev. The wing joint is essential so that the dish may be finished professionally with a cutlet frill. Order the breast and wing pieces in advance from the butcher.

**SERVING IDEAS**
Serve Chicken Kiev with crisp, golden fried straw potatoes and peas in pastry boats or round tartlets. Alternatively, serve the chicken with creamed spinach flavoured with freshly ground nutmeg, and croquette potatoes.

● 535 calories/2250 kj per portion

**VARIATIONS**
Strongly flavoured garlic butter is an integral part of Chicken Kiev; the quantity of garlic may be varied. However, if you do not care for garlic, try a variation of the dish: use 1 tablespoon finely snipped chives instead. Alternatively the butter may be flavoured with 1 tablespoon finely chopped fresh parsley and a seasoning of onion salt to taste.

**WATCHPOINTS**
Chilling the garlic butter for at least 4 hours is essential: it must be ice cold and quite firm so that it melts slowly as the chicken is frying.
The frying temperature is critical: if the oil is too hot, the coating will overbrown before the chicken is cooked.
Be sure to provide table napkins when serving Chicken Kiev: the liquid butter tends to spurt out when the chicken breast is cut.

## MAKING A 'POCKET' IN THE CHICKEN

**1** *Make a slit horizontally to within 2.5 cm/1 inch of each end.*

**2** *Insert a finger of chilled garlic butter lengthways into pocket.*

**3** *Press the edges of pocket firmly together to enclose butter.*

*Pashka* means Easter in Russian, and is the name given to the sweet, creamy pudding with dried fruits and almonds traditionally served in Russia at Easter. *Pashka* is eaten after the Russian Orthodox midnight Easter service in which the congregation celebrates the Resurrection of Christ, amidst glorious singing and a blaze of candles.

The *pashka* pudding was originally made in a pyramid-shaped wooden mould carved with the Russian letters XB (standing for *Christos voskrese*, 'Christ is risen' in Russian), the Russian Orthodox cross and the Easter symbols of an egg, and a cockerel. It was eaten with *kulich*, a sweet yeast bread which was served surrounded by brightly coloured Easter eggs.

*Pashka* is very rich, containing eggs, cream and butter, ingredients forbidden by the Russian Church during Lent. In flavour and texture *pashka* is rather like cheesecake. Tea, served Russian-style in glasses, without milk and with a slice of lemon if liked, goes well with it.

## Pashka

SERVES 6-8
750 g/1½ lb curd cheese
100 g/4 oz unsalted butter, softened
3 eggs, separated
100 g/4 oz caster sugar
3 tablespoons double cream
½ vanilla pod
50 g/2 oz blanched almonds, chopped
75 g/3 oz seedless raisins

TO DECORATE
cut mixed peel
glacé cherries and angelica
whole blanched almonds

1 Cut out a large piece of scalded muslin or cheesecloth to line a 15 cm/6 inch diameter flowerpot (see Step 1).
2 Using a wooden spoon, beat the curd cheese and butter together in a bowl until very smooth. Set aside.
3 Put the egg yolks and sugar in a separate bowl. Whisk with a balloon whisk until thick and creamy.
4 Put the cream and vanilla pod in a small, heavy-based saucepan and bring slowly to just below boiling point. Remove the vanilla pod.
5 Allow the cream to cool very slightly, then pour slowly on to the egg mixture, beating constantly.
6 With a large metal spoon, fold the egg and cream mixture into the cheese and butter mixture. Fold in the almonds and raisins, so that they are evenly distributed.
7 Whisk egg whites until standing in stiff peaks and fold into mixture.
8 Carefully pour the mixture into the prepared flowerpot (see Step 2). Fold the cloth over, place a plate on top and weight down.
9 Put the flowerpot on a wire rack in a shallow dish so as much liquid as possible drains from *pashka* while setting. Refrigerate 24 hours.
10 Remove the weight and plate. To unmould, invert a round serving plate on top of the flowerpot, then gently invert, holding pot and plate firmly. Carefully remove the flowerpot and peel away the muslin.
11 Decorate the top and sides of the *pashka* with peel, cherries, angelica and almonds. Press gently but firmly into surface, so they adhere.

### PREPARING AND FILLING THE FLOWERPOT

1 *Line the flowerpot with scalded muslin or cheesecloth, pressing the cloth well into the edge round the base and leaving plenty of material round the edge to fold over the top.*

2 *Pour the pashka mixture into the lined flowerpot, then fold the edges of the cloth neatly over the top of the pot. Place a small plate inside the pot and weight down.*

## Cook's Notes

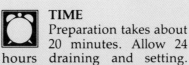

**TIME**
Preparation takes about 20 minutes. Allow 24 hours draining and setting. Finishing takes 15 minutes.

**SERVING IDEAS**
The *pashka* may be served as a pudding at the end of a meal, or for tea. The Italian yeast cake with dried fruits called *panettone*, available from Italian grocers and specialist food shops, is very like the Russian *kulich* with which *pashka* was traditionally served, and would make a good accompaniment. Or, serve the *pashka* with a light sponge cake.

**DID YOU KNOW**
The original Russian *pashka* contains considerably more sugar, and the egg whites are not whisked. It also needs 36 hours draining.

● 600 calories/2500 kj per portion

One of the delights of eating out Chinese style is the range of appetizing dishes on offer. Some of these, however, are deceptively simple to make and can quite easily be prepared at home.

Give your dining table a real flavour of the Orient by serving a dish of sweet and sour pork, accompanied by fried rice and stir-fried broccoli.

For Chinese fried rice, boil the rice for 15 minutes until not quite tender, drain and spread out to cool. Heat some vegetable oil in a large frying-pan and fry the rice, stirring constantly with a wooden spoon, for 3-5 minutes. Diced meat, shrimps and sliced vegetables stir-fried in the same way, make tasty and colourfully attractive additions to the rice.

For the table decoration, go Chinese and float single flower heads such as a chrysanthemum, dahlia or marguerite in small bowls of water. White flowers in white bowls look particularly elegant. And for a finishing touch, bring out the chopsticks!

## Chinese sweet and sour pork

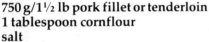

SERVES 4
750 g/1½ lb pork fillet or tenderloin
1 tablespoon cornflour
salt
vegetable oil, for deep-frying

SAUCE
1 teaspoon cornflour
4 tablespoons water
2 tablespoons wine or cider vinegar
2 tablespoons brown sugar
2 tablespoons orange juice
1 tablespoon tomato purée
2 tablespoons soy sauce
pinch of cayenne pepper
1 small onion, finely chopped
1 tablespoon vegetable oil
½ green pepper, deseeded and cut into thin strips
½ red pepper, deseeded and cut into thin strips

---

### MAKING SPRING ONION TASSELS

1 *Trim the spring onions of most of the green tops and remove the thin skin and the bulb end. With a small sharp knife, make several slits close together from top to bulb end of onion.*

2 *Place the onions in a bowl of iced water for 1 hour. The tops will curl back to make an attractive 'tassel'. Drain thoroughly and use to garnish the edge of the serving platter.*

---

1 To make the sauce: put the cornflour into a bowl and then gradually pour on the water, stirring all the time to form a smooth mixture. Stir in the vinegar, sugar, orange juice, tomato purée, soy sauce, cayenne pepper and half the chopped onion.

2 Trim away any excess fat from the pork and cut into 2.5 cm/1 inch cubes. Season the cornflour with a pinch of salt and put it into a grease-proof or polythene bag. Toss the meat cubes in it, a few at a time, to coat them thoroughly. Remove the meat and shake off any excess cornflour.

3 Heat the oil in a deep frying-pan to a temperature of 190C/375F on a cooking thermometer, or until a small cube of bread turns golden brown in 50 seconds. Fry half the meat for about 6-8 minutes, until it is crisp and golden brown.  Remove with a slotted spoon, drain it on crumpled absorbent paper and keep it warm while you fry the remainder of the meat.

4 Heat the tablespoon of vegetable oil in a frying-pan, add the remaining chopped onion and strips of green and red pepper. Fry over high heat for 1 minute, lower the heat to moderate, then pour in the sauce. Stir for a few minutes until the sauce is bubbling and thickened. Add the cooked cubes of pork and stir carefully. Cook for 1 minute only, to blend the flavours. Turn the meat and sauce into a warmed serving dish and serve at once.

### Cook's Notes

**TIME**
Preparation and cooking take 35 minutes.

**VARIATION**
Cubes of lamb or chicken can be cooked and stirred into the sauce in the same way. Small cubes of chicken will deep-fry in 5-6 minutes.

**WATCHPOINT**
Cook the meat in batches in a deep frying-pan — do not try to cook it all together in a small pan of oil because the meat will lower the temperature of the oil too much, and it will not cook to the characteristic crispness that is important in this dish.

●680 calories/2850 kj per portion

# Stir-fried broccoli

**SERVES 4**

500 g/1 lb frozen broccoli, defrosted
2 spring onions
2 tablespoons vegetable oil
½ teaspoon salt
1 tablespoon soy sauce
2 tablespoons dry sherry

**1** Drain the broccoli. Cut into 5 cm/ 2 inch strips and cut the stalks in half lengthways if thick.
**2** Slice the onions, discarding most of the green ends.
**3** Heat the oil in a large frying-pan. Add the onions and salt and fry over high heat for 30 seconds. Add the broccoli, lower the heat to moderate and stir for 3 minutes.
**4** Pour on the soy sauce and sherry. Continue to stir for 2 minutes until the vegetables and sauce are very hot. Serve at once.

## Cook's Notes

**TIME**
Cooking time is 10 minutes, but allow 1 hour for the broccoli to defrost.

**COOK'S TIP**
Use fresh broccoli if available. Cook it in boiling salted water for 3 minutes then drain thoroughly before stir-frying.

●85 calories/375 kj per portion

An essential principle of the ancient Chinese philosophy known as Taoism is that harmony arises from the proper blending of opposites (the *yin-yang* principle). This belief is also reflected in Chinese cooking, of which a main feature is the balance of colours, flavours and textures. This Cantonese recipe illustrates this harmony perfectly.

## Cook's Notes

### TIME
Preparation takes about 25 minutes, marinating 30 minutes and the cooking less than 5 minutes.

### COOK'S TIPS
Beat the steak between 2 sheets of greaseproof paper to tenderize as well as flatten it to the required thickness before cutting into strips.

1 tablespoon light soy sauce and 1 tablespoon rich soy sauce may be used, if liked, for a darker colour.

If the mange-tout peas are small, leave them whole – if they are large, it is better to cut them in half.

A wok with a long wooden handle is best for stir-frying (a two-handled wok is suitable for steaming).

### WATCHPOINTS
When stir-frying both the mange-tout and the beef, add the stock only if absolutely necessary: the dish should not be served in a thin, runny sauce.

Do not keep the mange-tout in the oven – they will lose their bright green colour.

### VARIATION
If mange-tout are not available, use a large green pepper, deseeded and finely shredded.

●190 calories/800 kj per portion

# Beef with mange-tout peas

**SERVES 4**

350 g/12 oz frying steak, cut across grain into 4 × 2.5 cm × 5 mm/1½ × 1 × ¼ inch strips (see Cook's tips)
1 tablespoon cornflour
1 tablespoon dry sherry
2 tablespoons light soy sauce (see Cook's tips)
1 teaspoon salt
1½ teaspoons sugar
4 tablespoons vegetable oil
250 g/9 oz mange-tout peas, topped and tailed (see Cook's tips and Variation)
1 tablespoon chicken stock (optional)
2 spring onions, finely chopped
2 slices fresh root ginger, finely chopped

1 In a large bowl, blend the cornflour with the sherry and soy sauce to a smooth paste. Add a pinch of the salt and 1 teaspoon of the sugar. Stir in the beef strips, then cover and leave to marinate for about 30 minutes stirring once. Meanwhile boil 12 oz/350 g rice to accompany the dish. Cool before stir-frying.

2 Heat a long-handled wok for 1½ minutes (see Cook's tips). Heat half the oil in the wok. When it is smoking, add the mange-tout peas, stir over brisk heat until evenly coated with oil, then add the remaining salt and sugar and stir-fry for 1-1½ minutes, adding a little chicken stock if the peas show signs of sticking. ⚠ Transfer the mange-tout peas to a warmed serving dish, cover and keep in a warm place while frying the beef. ⚠

3 Wash and dry the wok, heat it again, then add the remaining oil. Heat until smoking, then add the spring onions and ginger root and stir once.

4 Using a slotted spoon, lift the beef strips from the marinade, draining off any excess, and add to the wok. Stir over brisk heat until evenly coated with oil, then stir-fry for 1 minute, adding a little chicken stock if the beef shows any signs of sticking. Spoon the beef over the mange-tout and serve at once, accompanied by fried rice, handed round separately in a warmed serving bowl.

A popular and wonderfully tasty stir-fried mixture of meat and vegetables, *Chop suey* did not actually originate in China itself. It is believed to have been invented by pioneering Chinese restaurateurs in the United States at the height of the nineteenth-century Gold Rush.

# Chop suey

SERVES 4
**250 g/9 oz pork fillet, trimmed of excess fat**
**2 teaspoons cornflour**
**1 tablespoon dry sherry**
**2 tablespoons soy sauce**
**2 spring onions**
**2 slices fresh ginger root**
**½ cauliflower**
**2 carrots**
**1 small green pepper**
**100 g/4 oz fresh beansprouts (see Cook's tips)**
**3 tomatoes**
**5 tablespoons vegetable oil**
**1 teaspoon salt**
**1 teaspoon sugar**
**a little chicken stock (optional)**

**1** Cut the pork lengthways into four 2.5 cm/1½ inch slices, then cut each into slices about 5 mm/¼ inch thick. Place in a shallow dish.
**2** In a small bowl, blend together the cornflour, sherry and soy sauce to make a smooth paste. Pour the mixture over the pork, stir well to mix, then cover and leave to marinate while you prepare the vegetables.
**3** Cut the spring onions into 1 cm/½ inch strips. Peel and finely chop the ginger root. Break the cauliflower into florets, discarding the leaves and any thick fibrous stalks. Thinly slice the carrots. Deseed and finely shred the green pepper. Trim the beansprouts of any husks. Slice the tomatoes.
**4** Heat 3 tablespoons oil in a wok (see Cook's tips) or large frying-pan until it is just smoking. Add the sliced pork and stir with a long-handled spoon or spatula for 2-3 minutes until each slice is coated with oil. Transfer the pork slices to a plate with a slotted spoon.

## CLEANING A WOK

**1** *Always season a new wok before use: wash in hot water, dry over moderate heat and wipe inside with a pad of absorbent paper soaked in vegetable oil.*

**2** *After use, wash under hot water; do not use detergent. Brush or scour with soapless scourer, then dry thoroughly over moderate heat to prevent rusting.*

**5** Heat the remaining oil in the wok and add the spring onions and slices of fresh ginger root to flavour the oil.
**6** Add the cauliflower florets and sliced carrots to the wok and cook, stirring all the time, for 1 minute.
**7** Add the green pepper, beansprouts and tomatoes and cook, stirring all the time, for 1 further minute. Season with salt and sugar and stir a few more times until heated through.
**8** Add the pork slices, moisten with a little stock if necessary (see Cook's tips) and stir for 30 seconds. Taste and adjust seasoning, transfer to a warmed dish and serve at once (see Serving ideas).

## Cook's Notes

**TIME**
Preparation takes about 30 minutes, cooking only about 5 minutes.

**COOK'S TIPS**
Use fresh beansprouts for this recipe: canned ones are not crisp enough.
The advantage of stir-frying in a wok, with its sloping sides and rounded base, is that the heat is evenly distributed so only a short cooking time is required; the ingredients always return to the centre however vigorously you stir them. Woks should be heated before oil is put in them.
The ingredients should produce enough natural juices to form a kind of gravy, but if the contents of the wok are too dry, add a little stock and bring to the boil before serving.

**SERVING IDEAS**
Serve with boiled or fried rice and Chinese egg noodles.

**DID YOU KNOW**
Chop suey gets its name from the Chinese word *zasui* meaning mixed bits.
Preparation of the ingredients is very important in Chinese cooking. Traditionally, all the chopping of the vegetables for a chop suey is done while the meat is marinating.

**VARIATIONS**
Chicken breast or lean rump or frying steak are good replacements for pork.

●290 calories/1225 kj per portion

# JAPAN

The idea of frying food was introduced to Japan by the Portuguese in the 16th century, and *tempura* — pieces of fish, shellfish, meat and vegetables coated in a light batter, deep fried and served with a tasty sauce — is now one of Japan's favourite dishes. Tempura is a perfect example of the Japanese taste for cooking food quickly, in order to help preserve the naturally fresh, delicate flavour of the ingredients.

In Japan's climate the four seasons are very distinct, and each of them has it own characteristic foods. The Japanese like to include at least one seasonal ingredient in *tempura*. They might include bamboo shoots for spring; okra or asparagus for summer; chrysanthemum or maple leaves for autumn and sweet potato for winter.

# Tempura

**SERVES 4**

**12 prawns, body shell removed and tails left on (see Steps)**
**4 mushrooms, stalks removed**
**1 large carrot, cut into sticks**
**1 large green pepper, deseeded and cut into 8 pieces**
**1 onion, cut into 5 mm/¼ inch slices**
**600 ml/1 pint sunflower oil, for deep frying (see Cook's tips)**

**SAUCE**
**150 ml/¼ pint Japanese soup stock (see Buying guide) or water**
**2 tablespoons soy sauce**
**pinch of salt**
**2 teaspoons sugar**
**100 g/4 oz white radish (see Buying guide), finely grated**

**BATTER**
**100 g/4 oz plain flour, sifted**
**1 egg, lightly beaten**
**175 ml/6 fl oz cold water**

**1** Make the sauce: stir together all the ingredients except the radish in a small saucepan. Bring to the boil, remove from heat and set aside.
**2** Make the batter: in a bowl quickly mix together all the ingredients (see Cook's tips) until blended.
**3** Heat the oil in a deep-fat frier to 180C/350F or until a bread cube browns in 60 seconds.
**4** Quickly dip the ingredients in the batter and fry in batches, starting with the vegetables (see Cook's tips), until puffed and golden.
**5** Transfer to individual plates (see Did you know).
**6** Stir the radish into sauce in the pan, pour into 4 individual small bowls and serve at once with the tempura (see Cook's tips).

## Cook's Notes

**TIME**
Preparation takes about 30 minutes and frying about 10 minutes.

**COOK'S TIPS**
Sunflower oil gives the best flavour to tempura; corn oil is also suitable.

Mixing the batter quickly ensures that the tempura has a light, crisp thin batter coating through which the colours of the food can be seen. Over-stirring makes the batter heavy and gives a 'bready' result. In Japan the batter is mixed with bamboo cooking chopsticks.

Fry the vegetables first, to ensure that they do not have a fishy taste. Fry only enough ingredients at once to cover half the surface of the oil: if too many are fried the temperature of the oil is lowered and the food will not cook properly.

Tempura is best eaten as soon as it is fried, so be sure to have everything ready to serve when it is cooked.

**BUYING GUIDE**
Japanese food stores sell instant soup stock (called *dashinomoto*), made from kelp and flaked dried bonito fish. Dissolve 1 tablespoon in 150 ml/¼ pint water for a very tasty sauce.

There are a number of varieties of radish apart from the familiar red-skinned salad radishes. White radish is a long tapering root which probably originated in southern Asia: in Japan a variety called *daikon* radish is widely used in cooking – grated as a garnish and in sauces, sliced in vegetable mixtures and pickled to eat with various kinds of fish.

White radish is sold in oriental food stores. There is a similar vegetable called mooli. If you cannot obtain either, use grated horseradish.

**DID YOU KNOW**
In Japan, plates or racks of meshed bamboo are often used for serving tempura, lined with special absorbent tempura paper which is sold ready-cut to size in packets.

It is usual in Japan to serve food on individual plates, not from a serving platter: this is an extension of a past tradition when the diners used to sit at separate tables.

A Japanese meal normally consists of 4 or 5 dishes which are served at the same time and eaten in no particular order. The selection might consist of a main dish such as tempura or raw fish, pickled vegetables, rice and soup. Sake (Japanese rice wine), beer or white wine would be served with the meal.

●250 calories/1050 kj per portion

## REMOVING BODY SHELL FROM A PRAWN

**1** *Straighten the prawn as much as possible and then pull off the head with a twisting movement.*

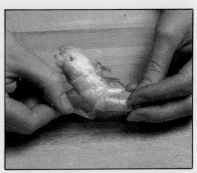

**2** *Insert fingers under the legs and pull upwards over the saddle to remove shell and leave tail intact.*

# INDONESIA

*Saté*, the Malay word for spiced sauce, is also the name of one of the most popular of all dishes eaten in Indonesia. A saté consists of marinated cubes of meat threaded on to skewers, grilled and served with a spicy peanut sauce on a bed of rice.

## Chicken saté with peanut sauce

**SERVES 4**

4 large chicken leg pieces, each weighing about 350 g/12 oz
1 small onion, very finely chopped
1 small green pepper, deseeded and very finely chopped
3 tablespoons soy sauce
2 tablespoons lemon juice
1 tablespoon vegetable oil
1 teaspoon dark soft brown sugar

**PEANUT SAUCE**

40 g/1½ oz desiccated coconut
225 ml/8 fl oz boiling water
5 tablespoons crunchy peanut butter
2 teaspoons dark soft brown sugar
½ teaspoon chilli powder

**1** Cut the chicken into bite-sized pieces, discarding skin and bones (see Steps, below, and Economy). Put the chicken in a bowl.

**2** Mix the chopped onion with the green pepper, soy sauce, lemon juice, oil and brown sugar. Pour the mixture over the chicken, stir well, then leave to marinate in a cool place for at least 2 hours, turning the meat occasionally.

**3** Meanwhile, prepare the sauce: put the coconut into a bowl and pour over the boiling water. Cover with a saucer or plate and leave to stand for 15 minutes. Strain into a small saucepan, pressing all the liquid out of the coconut with the backs of your fingers. Discard the coconut. Add the remaining sauce ingredients to the pan, mix well and set aside.

**4** Heat the grill to moderate.

**5** Drain the chicken reserving the marinade. Thread the chicken on to 4 oiled long skewers, leaving a slight gap between each piece. Remove the rack from the grill pan, place the skewers in the pan and pour over 2-3 tablespoons marinade.

**6** Grill for about 15 minutes, turning and basting occasionally with more marinade until cooked through. Remove from the grill and keep hot.

**7** Add all the marinade and the juices from the grill pan to the peanut sauce. Bring to the boil, stirring, then simmer for 1-2 minutes.

**8** To serve: put the saté on a bed of yellow rice and hand the sauce separately. Serve at once.

## Cook's Notes

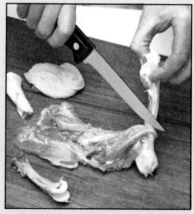

**TIME**
Total preparation time about 1 hour, marinating 2 hours, cooking 15 minutes, including cooking rice.

**ECONOMY**
Save the chicken bones for making stock.

**FOR CHILDREN**
Use pepper, not chilli powder in the sauce.

●450 calories/1875 kj per portion

---

### BONING THE CHICKEN

**1** *Put the chicken piece on a board. Using a sharp knife, cut off the bottom scaly leg joint, if necessary.*

**2** *Pull away skin and fat, then turn fleshy side down. Slit leg flesh through to bone. Ease leg flesh away from bone.*

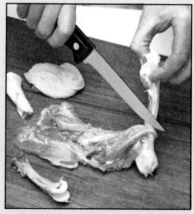

**3** *Break the 2 leg joints and pull out the leg bones. Ease remaining meat from bones and discard them or use for stock.*

# INDIA

The Indonesians are especially fond of salads made from lightly cooked, crisp and crunchy vegetables. Peanuts feature prominently in Indonesian cooking, and *Gado-gado*—which means 'a mixture'—is topped with a nutty savoury sauce. It is one of the most popular dishes throughout the Indonesian islands.

# Gado-gado

**SERVES 4**

1 potato, scrubbed but unpeeled
100 g/4 oz green cabbage or spring greens, shredded
100 g/4 oz French beans, sliced
100 g/4 oz carrots, thinly sliced
½ cauliflower, divided into florets
1 bunch of watercress, divided into sprigs
100 g/4 oz beansprouts

SAUCE
100 g/4 oz shelled raw peanuts (see Buying guide)
vegetable oil, for frying
1 clove garlic, crushed
2 shallots or ½ small onion, finely chopped
salt
½ teaspoon chilli powder
½ teaspoon light soft brown sugar
350 ml/12 fl oz water
juice of 1 lemon

TO GARNISH
1 large egg, hard-boiled and cut into wedges
1 lettuce, shredded
¼ cucumber, sliced
1 onion, sliced into rings and fried until crisp and brown
prawn crackers, fried (see Buying guide)

**1** Make the sauce: heat enough oil in a large, heavy frying-pan or wok to cover the peanuts. Add the peanuts and fry over moderate heat for 5-6 minutes, stirring occasionally. Remove the peanuts with a slotted spoon and drain on absorbent paper. Leave to cool. Pour all but 1 teaspoon of the oil out of the pan.
**2** Grind the cooled peanuts to a fine powder in a food processor or coffee grinder, or pound them, using a pestle and mortar.
**3** Reheat the oil in the pan, add the garlic and shallots, season with salt and fry for 1 minute. Stir in the chilli powder and sugar and add the water. Bring the mixture to the boil, then stir in the ground peanuts. Lower the heat and simmer, stirring occasionally, for 4-6 minutes until the sauce thickens. Set aside.
**4** Bring 3 saucepans of salted water to the boil. Add the potato to one pan and boil gently for 15 minutes.
**5** Meanwhile, add the cabbage, French beans, carrots and cauliflower to another pan and boil gently for 4 minutes.
**6** Add the watercress and bean-sprouts to the third pan and boil gently for 2-3 minutes.
**7** Drain all the vegetables very thoroughly. Allow the potato to cool slightly, then cut into thin slices.
**8** Pile the cabbage, French beans, carrots, cauliflower, watercress and beansprouts on to a round serving dish (see Cook's tip). Arrange the potato slices and hard-boiled egg wedges on top, and arrange the shredded lettuce and sliced cucumber round the edge.
**9** Stir the lemon juice into the sauce in the pan and heat through gently. Pour the sauce over the salad. Garnish with fried onion rings and prawn crackers, broken into small pieces. Serve at once.

## Cook's Notes

**TIME**
Preparing the vegetables takes 20-30 minutes. Making the sauce and cooking the vegetables take about 45 minutes. Assembling the salad and reheating the sauce take about 10 minutes.

**BUYING GUIDE**
Buy raw peanuts: roasted or salted peanuts will not give the right flavour or texture.
Prawn crackers, made from rice flour and prawns, are available in packets from Chinese food shops, oriental delicatessens and some large supermarkets: fry them according to packet instructions. Or use prawn-flavoured potato crisps instead for the garnish.

**SERVING IDEAS**
Gado-gado makes a delicious starter or side salad to accompany a fairly light main-course dish. Try it with fish, chicken or stir-fried pork.
With extra potato and egg added, Gado-gado makes an excellent snack lunch.

**DID YOU KNOW**
If you are serving Gado-gado with fish, and would like to give the sauce a seafood flavour, try adding a shrimp paste called *terasi*, available from Chinese food shops. It is very highly flavoured and needs to be used sparingly: crush a piece about the size of a hazelnut and fry it with the shallots and garlic.
You can make an 'instant' sauce for Gado-gado using *satay powder* from Chinese food shops.

**COOK'S TIP**
The salad is best served with the vegetables still just warm.

●335 calories/1400 kj per portion

# Yellow rice

**SERVES 4**
350 g/12 oz long-grain rice
2 tablespoons vegetable oil
 1 teaspoon ground turmeric
700 ml/1¼ pints chicken stock
¼ teaspoon ground cinnamon
1 bay leaf

**1** Heat the oil in a saucepan, add the rice and stir over moderate heat for 2 minutes. Add the turmeric, lower the heat and cook, stirring, for a further 1-2 minutes.
**2** Pour in the stock, [!] add the cinnamon and bay leaf and stir well.

**3** Bring to the boil, then lower the heat and cover with a tight-fitting lid. Cook over the lowest possible heat for 15 minutes or until all the liquid has been absorbed and the rice is tender. [!] Remove the bay leaf and serve hot.

## Cook's Notes

**TIME**
20 minutes to simmer and cook the rice.

**SERVING IDEAS**
Serve a cool cucumber relish with the saté: mix together a peeled, thinly sliced cucumber with 2 sliced spring onions, juice of 1 lemon, sugar and pepper to taste.

**WATCHPOINTS**
Stand well back when you add the stock to the pan of sautéed rice: the mixture will splutter and spit.
The rice must cook over the lowest heat, or the liquid evaporates too fast and the rice becomes dry before it is cooked.

●395 calories/1650 kj per portion

Madras beef curry, which is as hot and colourful as the region of Madras itself, was developed by the Moslems and Christians of southern India (Hindus, to whom the cow is sacred, never eat beef). Lime pickle is the traditional accompaniment – its tartness cleverly offsetting the rich spiciness of the beef.

# Madras beef curry

**SERVES 4**

750 g/1½ lb best-quality stewing steak, cut into 2.5 cm/1 inch cubes (see Buying guide)
4 tablespoons ghee
1 onion, thinly sliced
2 cloves garlic, finely chopped
2 teaspoons coriander seeds
2 teaspoons ground turmeric
1 teaspoon chilli powder
1 teaspoon ground coriander
1 teaspoon ground cumin
1 teaspoon freshly ground black pepper
7.5 cm/3 inch piece fresh root ginger, finely chopped
600 ml/1 pint boiling water
4 green chillies, cut into 5 mm/ ¼ inch pieces (see Cook's tips and Watchpoint)
1 teaspoon salt
2 teaspoons garam masala
coriander leaves and lime slices, to garnish

1 Melt the ghee in a large, heavy-based saucepan, add the beef cubes and fry over moderate heat, turning, to seal and brown on all sides. Remove the beef cubes with a slotted spoon, transfer them to a plate and set aside while preparing the spicy sauce.
2 Add the onion to the pan and fry gently for 5 minutes until soft and lightly coloured. Add the garlic, coriander seeds, turmeric, chilli powder, ground coriander and cumin, pepper and ginger. Add 4 tablespoons of the boiling water and stir well.
3 Add the beef cubes to the pan and stir well to coat with the spice mixture. Pour in the remaining water, add the chopped chillies and stir well again. Cover the saucepan and simmer for 45-60 minutes, until the beef is tender when pierced with a sharp knife (see Cook's tips). Add the salt and garam masala and stir well to mix.
4 Transfer the beef to a warmed serving dish, garnish with coriander leaves and lime slices and serve at once (see Serving ideas).

# Hot lime pickle

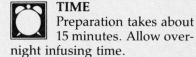

thinly pared zest and juice of 3-4 limes (total weight 250 g/9 oz)
1 tablespoon vegetable oil
1 tablespoon white wine vinegar
1 tablespoon chilli powder
1 teaspoon ground turmeric
2 green chillies, finely chopped

1 Put all the ingredients except the lime zest into a blender or food processor. Work for a few seconds until the mixture is smooth and thoroughly blended.
2 Cut the lime zest into matchstick strips and put them into a 1 kg/2 lb screw-top jar. Pour over the sauce, cover tightly with the lid and shake the jar well. Leave the hot lime pickle in a cool place overnight to allow the flavours to develop before serving with the curry (see Storage).

## Cook's Notes

### Beef curry

**TIME**
Preparation, including the pre-cooking, takes about 25 minutes. Cooking then takes 45-60 minutes.

**SERVING IDEAS**
Serve with plain boiled fluffy white rice, fried or grilled poppadoms and hot lime pickle (see recipe). Cold lager or beer is the ideal drink to accompany this spicy, hot Madras beef curry.

**! WATCHPOINT**
Wash your hands as soon as you have finished chopping the chillies: the juice can sting the eyes quite badly should you happen to rub them.

**COOK'S TIPS**
Most heat from chillies is in the seeds. For a milder curry remove the seeds from chillies during preparation, then rinse chillies.
According to the age and therefore the dryness of the spices, different amounts of water will be absorbed. Add a little more boiling water if the dish shows signs of becoming dry. The sauce should be fairly thick: if necessary, once the beef is cooked, increase the heat and cook, uncovered, until the liquid is reduced.

**BUYING GUIDE**
Chuck or flank are both suitable for this recipe.

●470 calories/1950 kj per portion

### Hot lime pickle

**TIME**
Preparation takes about 15 minutes. Allow overnight infusing time.

**COOK'S TIP**
Pickles made from limes, mangoes or chillies are extremely popular with Indians. The sharpness of these fruits helps counteract the hot taste of the curry.

**STORAGE**
Although the pickle can be served within 1 day of making, the flavour will improve with storing. The pickle will keep for up to 3 months in the refrigerator.

●35 calories/150 kj per portion

The *korma* is widely regarded as a superior example of Indian cuisine, far from any run-of-the-mill curry dish. Containing a number of luxurious ingredients—saffron, poppy seeds, cashew nuts and cream—*kormas* are mostly reserved for feast days and holidays.

# Chicken korma

SERVES 4

1.5 kg/3-3½ lb oven-ready chicken, divided into 8 pieces and skin removed (see Step)
1 lemon, halved
1 tablespoon salt
275 g/10 oz natural yoghurt
½ teaspoon saffron threads
1 tablespoon poppy seeds
5 cm/2 inch cinnamon stick, broken into small pieces
1 teaspoon chilli powder
1 teaspoon dried coriander seeds
1 teaspoon ground cumin
½ teaspoon black pepper
2 tablespoons water
4 tablespoons ghee or vegetable oil (see Buying Guide, page 113)
1 onion, thinly sliced
1 clove garlic, crushed
5 cm/2 inch piece fresh root ginger, cut into thin strips
10 cardamom pods
10 cloves
50 g/2 oz unsalted cashew nuts
150 ml/¼ pint double cream
coriander leaves, to garnish

1 Rub the chicken with the lemon. Squeeze the juice over a bowl large enough to hold the chicken and yoghurt.
2 Put the chicken pieces in the bowl and sprinkle with the salt. Pour over the yoghurt and turn the chicken pieces to coat thoroughly. Cover and leave to marinate for 2 hours.
3 Crush the saffron threads in your fingers. Drop them into a tea cup and half-fill with boiling water. Leave to soak for at least 2 hours to release colour and flavour, then strain the liquid.
4 Put the poppy seeds, cinnamon, chilli powder, coriander seeds, cumin and pepper with the water

into a coffee grinder (see Cook's tip) or the goblet of a blender and work for 1-2 minutes until thoroughly combined into a spicy paste.
5 Melt the ghee in a large saucepan. Add the onion and fry gently for about 3 minutes. ! Add the garlic and ginger and fry for a further 2 minutes. Stir in the spicy paste, add the cardamom pods and cloves and cook for a further 1 minute.
6 Add the chicken pieces to the pan, together with the yoghurt and the strained saffron liquid. Heat to just below boiling and cover tightly. Simmer very gently for 1½ hours.
7 Stir in the cashew nuts and cream and simmer for a further 15 minutes. Transfer to a warmed serving dish, garnish with coriander and serve.

## TO SKIN CHICKEN

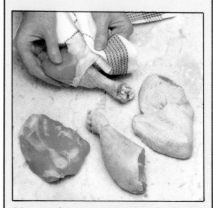

*Use a clean tea towel to hold the skin as you pull it away from the flesh, to give a firmer grip.*

## Cook's Notes

**TIME**
Allow 2 hours marinating and soaking the saffron. Preparation, including pre-cooking, takes 15 minutes. Cooking the *korma* takes a total of 1¾ hours.

**WATCHPOINT**
Do not overcook the onions at this stage. They should be softened but not browned. All the colour in the dish should come from the bright golden saffron.

**SERVING IDEAS**
Boiled rice is good with Chicken *korma*, but for a change serve *naan*—the flat leavened bread that is traditionally baked in India in the tandoor clay oven. *Naan* bread is available from Indian and Greek specialist food stores. Or, try one of the range of instant Indian bread mixes now available from large supermarkets.

**COOK'S TIPS**
If you do a lot of Indian cooking, it is well worth keeping a coffee grinder specially for grinding the spices which are the essential feature of this cuisine, or invest in a mortar and pestle to work the spices. Both methods will release the essential oils of the spices.

**BUYING GUIDE**
If you cannot find fresh ginger, available from supermarkets and oriental stores, use ½ teaspoon ground ginger instead.

**DID YOU KNOW**
Chicken *korma* was originally made with yoghurt only, giving a dish with less sauce – *korma* means 'dry'. As cream became more widely used in India, it was added to increase the richness of a dish.

● 605 calories/2525 kj per portion

*Rogan Josh* is a spiced lamb dish which is popular throughout the Muslim areas of Northern India and the North West Frontier — each region having its own version. *Sag Aloo*, a delicious spicy blend of spinach and chunky potatoes, is a popular vegetable accompaniment.

# Rogan Josh

SERVES 4

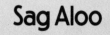

750 g/1½ lb boned leg or shoulder of lamb, cubed (see Buying guide)
3 tablespoons ghee or vegetable oil (see Buying guide)
8 whole black peppercorns
3 cloves
4 cardamom seeds
1 whole dried chilli pepper (optional)
1 tablespoon desiccated coconut
3 tablespoons ground almonds
2 tablespoons ground coriander
1 tablespoon ground cumin
1 teaspoon ground turmeric
¼ teaspoon freshly grated nutmeg
¼ teaspoon ground mace
8 tablespoons water
2.5 cm/1 inch piece fresh root ginger, peeled and finely chopped
2 cloves garlic, crushed
1 onion, very finely chopped
1 teaspoon salt
3 tablespoons natural yoghurt
225 g/8 oz can tomatoes

1 Heat 2 tablespoons of ghee in a large saucepan, add peppercorns, cloves, cardamom seeds and the chilli pepper, if using, and fry over moderate heat for 1-2 minutes until they start to darken.

2 Add the meat and fry for 5 minutes to brown on all sides. Remove from the heat, drain off and reserve any liquid. Set aside the liquid and the meat.

3 Heat the grill to high. In a bowl mix together the coconut, almonds, coriander and cumin. Spread out in the grill pan and grill until the mixture starts to brown. Stir once or twice to brown evenly. Transfer the mixture to a bowl and mix in the turmeric, nutmeg, mace, the reserved liquid from the meat and the water and set aside.

4 Heat the remaining ghee in a frying-pan, add ginger and garlic and fry gently for 1-2 minutes. Add the onion and cook for about 5 minutes until soft and lightly coloured.

5 Stir in the coconut and spice paste and cook for 2 minutes, stirring constantly. Add the salt, yoghurt and the tomatoes and their juice. Bring to the boil, lower the heat and simmer for 5 minutes.

6 Pour the mixture over the meat and spices in the saucepan and stir well. Bring to the boil, then lower the heat and simmer gently for about 1¼-1½ hours, stirring the meat and sauce occasionally.

7 Remove the dried chilli pepper, if used, and transfer Rogan Josh to warmed serving dish. Serve at once with Sag Aloo (see recipe).

# Sag Aloo

SERVES 4

400 g/14 oz can spinach
250 g/9 oz potatoes, cut into chunks
2 tablespoons ghee or vegetable oil
6 whole black peppercorns
2 cardamom seeds
1 fresh red chilli, deseeded and finely shredded
2.5 cm/1 inch fresh root ginger, peeled and cut into small sticks
½ onion, sliced
1 clove garlic, crushed
1 teaspoon ground coriander
1 teaspoon ground cumin
salt
3 tablespoons water

1 Heat the ghee in a saucepan, add the peppercorns and cardamom seeds and fry for 2-3 minutes.

2 Add the chilli, ginger, onion and garlic to the pan and cook for a further 3-4 minutes.

3 Stir in the spices and salt and mix well. Add the potatoes and the water. Bring to the boil, then lower the heat and simmer for 5 minutes, stirring occasionally.

4 Gently stir in the spinach, then simmer for about 30 minutes until potatoes are tender.

# Cook's Notes

## Rogan Josh

**TIME**
Preparation takes about 30 minutes and cooking 1¼-1½ hours. The dish can be prepared in advance to the end of stage 5. Leave to stand after adding the cooked paste, yoghurt and tomatoes to meat.

**COOK'S TIP**
The flavour of spices varies according to the way they are prepared: quickly frying the whole spices and toasting the ground spices gives the authentic Indian taste to this delicious lamb dish.

**WATCHPOINT**
Take great care when toasting the nuts and spices under the grill as they brown very quickly. As soon as they begin to colour, stir with a wooden spoon to brown the nuts and spices underneath.

●565 calories/2375 kj per portion

**BUYING GUIDE**
You will need about 1 kg/2-2½ lb meat on the bone to get 750 g/1½ lb lean meat. A small leg is the best cut for this recipe as it has far less fat than a shoulder.

Ghee is an Indian cooking fat which can be made either from clarified butter or vegetable fat. It is easily obtainable from specialist Indian grocers.

**DID YOU KNOW**
Outside India spiced dishes like these are known as curries, derived from the Tamil word *kari*, meaning 'a sauce'. In India each dish is known by its own name.

**SERVING IDEAS**
Serve with Sag Aloo, boiled rice, a selection of chutneys and relishes and raita: mix 275 g/10 oz natural yoghurt with peeled grated cucumber, seasoned with salt and black pepper. Serve with mango

chutney, hot lime pickle, tomato relish, grated carrot and banana salad, and chopped onions mixed with chilli powder.

## Sag Aloo

**TIME**
Preparing and cooking take about 45 minutes. The Sag Aloo can be prepared and cooked after the Rogan Josh has started to cook.

**VARIATION**
Frozen spinach can be used in place of canned. Substitute two 250 g/9 oz packs frozen chopped spinach. Leave to thaw, retaining all the liquid. Add a little more water if the Sag Aloo shows signs of drying out during cooking.

**SERVING IDEAS**
This spicy vegetable dish can be served with any curried meat dish.

●135 calories/550 kj per portion

Carpetbag steak, thick-cut beef steak stuffed with oysters, was very popular in Victorian England. It travelled successfully with the early settlers to Australia, where the abundance of prime beef and large juicy oysters established it as a firm favourite. Today it is still a much-appreciated dinner-party dish in Australia, and is excellent stuffed with mussels—as here—which are much less expensive than oysters.

## Carpet bag steak

**SERVES 4**

750 g/1½ lb rump steak, in one piece, about 5 cm/2 inches thick, trimmed of excess fat (see Buying guide)
24 fresh mussels (see Buying guide)
75 ml/3 fl oz water
75 ml/3 fl oz dry white wine
salt and freshly ground black pepper
2 sprigs fresh thyme or ½ teaspoon dried thyme
2 leaves fresh sage or ½ teaspoon dried sage
2 tablespoons vegetable oil
1 tablespoon lemon juice
1 tablespoon chopped fresh parsley
1 tablespoon dry sherry

1 Prepare the mussels: remove the beards, scrub the shells well and discard any that are opened.
2 Cook the mussels: place them in a large saucepan with the water and wine. Bring to the boil, cover and cook over high heat for 4-5 minutes, shaking the pan often, until all the shells are opened (see Watchpoint page 55). Drain and leave until cool enough to handle, then prise the mussels out of the shells with a small, very sharp knife. Pat dry with absorbent paper.
3 Season the steak with salt and pepper. Fill the pocket with the drained cooked mussels and secure the edges of the steak with wooden cocktail sticks.
4 Place the thyme and sage in a shallow earthenware dish and carefully lay the mussel-stuffed steak on top. Mix the oil with the lemon juice and pour over the steak. Leave to marinate for at least 1 hour, turning

the steak in the herb marinade after 30 minutes.
5 Heat the oven to 110C/225F/Gas ¼. Heat the grill to moderate.
6 Lift the steak from the marinade and lay it on the grill rack. Grill the steak, basting often with the marinade mixture and turning it carefully with kitchen tongs halfway through cooking time, until done to your liking: 8 minutes on each side for rare meat; 10-12 minutes for medium meat; 15 minutes for well done meat.
7 When the steak is cooked, transfer to a warmed serving dish then remove and discard the cocktail sticks. Keep the grilled steak hot in the oven.
8 Turn the grill to high. Add the parsley and sherry to the juices in the grill pan and heat quickly under the grill. Pour the juices over the cooked steak.
9 Serve the steak hot, cut into slices so that there is a portion of mussel filling in each slice.

**PREPARING STEAK FOR STUFFING**

*Make a pocket in the steak by slitting horizontally: cut through one long edge and to within 1 cm/ ½ inch of the other 3 edges.*

## Cook's Notes

**TIME**
Allow 2-3 hours defrosting time if using frozen mussels. Cooking the mussels takes about 5 minutes, stuffing the steak about 5 minutes. Allow 1 hour marinating time. Cooking then takes about 15-30 minutes and finishing the dish about 3 minutes.

**BUYING GUIDE**
Ask your butcher for well-hung middle cut of rump steak, about 5 cm/2 inches thick. Ask him to cut a deep pocket for the mussel stuffing by slitting the steak lengthways, starting at one long edge and cutting through to within not more than 1 cm/½ inch of the other 3 edges. This is a fairly delicate operation, requiring considerable skill and a razor-sharp knife, and if you are unsure then ask the butcher to prepare the pocket for you.
If fresh mussels are not available, use a 225 g/8 oz can, well drained, or ready-cooked frozen shelled mussels (sold as 'mussel meats'), thoroughly defrosted.

**SERVING IDEAS**
In the Australian tradition, serve this steak at a barbecue with a green salad and buttered jacket potatoes — allow a few minutes less to cook the steak. Australian wines are becoming increasingly available and make a good accompaniment to this dish.

●305 calories/1275 kj per portion

**Pavlova was created and named by a society hostess in honour of the famous ballerina Anna Pavlova during a tour of Australia. One of Australia's favourite national dishes, it is a wonderfully light and rich combination of meringue, whipped cream and fruit. Perfect for a special dinner party, it is, however, so popular with the Australians that they would be just as likely to serve it for an informal barbecue in the garden for family or friends.**

In Australia, Pavlova is often filled with juicy, orange-yellow passion fruit, which is readily available, but it is just as successful filled with other fruits such as strawberries, ripe peaches and kiwi fruit which have soft textures and bright colours to contrast with the meringue.

A less well-known version, but one that is equally popular in Australia, is Lemon Pavlova, in which the meringue case is exactly the same as the traditional Pavlova, but the fruit and cream are replaced by a tangy lemon filling which makes a lovely piquant contrast to the sweetness of the meringue. It also provides an excellent way of using up the egg yolks (left over from the meringue) and is more suited to winter climates when soft fruits are not available. If you prefer the fruit and cream filling, however, simply make the meringue case as below and fill with 300 ml/½ pint sweetened whipped cream and the fruits of your choice.

## Pavlova

SERVES 6
**MERINGUE CASE**
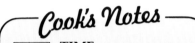
**4 large egg whites (see Watchpoints)**
**¼ teaspoon salt**
**100 g/4 oz granulated sugar**
**100 g/4 oz caster sugar**
**1 teaspoon cornflour**
**½ teaspoon vinegar**
**lemon zest, to decorate**

**LEMON FILLING**
**4 large egg yolks**
**50 g/2 oz caster sugar**
**4 tablespoons lemon juice**
**1 tablespoon grated lemon zest**
**175 ml/6 fl oz whipping cream**

1 Heat the oven to 110C/225F/Gas ¼.
2 With a pencil, lightly draw a 20 cm/8 inch circle on a sheet of non-stick vegetable parchment paper or foil. Place on a baking sheet or cut out first (see Steps).
3 Make the meringue case: put the egg whites into a large bowl making sure that it is spotlessly clean and thoroughly dry.
4 With a balloon whisk, whisk the egg whites and salt until standing in stiff peaks (see Steps). Gradually whisk in the granulated sugar, 1 tablespoon at a time, whisking until the sugar is thoroughly dissolved.
5 Sift the caster sugar with the cornflour and, using a metal spoon, fold mixture into the whisked egg whites. Finally, fold in the vinegar.
6 Spread a 2 cm/¾ inch layer of meringue evenly over the circle drawn on the paper, on the baking sheet. Build the rest of the meringue up to form the sides of the case, using a spoon or a piping bag fitted with a large plain nozzle.
7 Bake the meringue case in the oven for 1½-2 hours until the meringue is crisp and just very lightly coloured.
8 Meanwhile, make the filling: whisk the egg yolks in a bowl until foamy. Slowly beat in the caster sugar, then the lemon juice and zest. Transfer to the top of a double boiler or a flameproof bowl set snugly over a saucepan of simmering water. Stir until the mixture is thick and smooth; it is ready when it slides cleanly straight from the spoon, without trickling. (This is a slow process and can take as long as 10 minutes.) Leave until quite cold.
9 When the meringue is baked, remove from the oven and leave to cool slightly, then very carefully peel away the paper from the base. Place the meringue case on a flat

serving plate to cool completely, ready for filling.
10 When both meringue and lemon filling are cold, whip the cream until thick and fold into lemon filling. Spoon into centre of the meringue case, top with a little lemon zest and serve at room temperature.

*Cook's Notes*

 **TIME**
Preparing the meringue case takes about 45 minutes; making the filling and baking the meringue takes 1½-2 hours. Both the meringue and the filling require a further 30 minutes to cool.

**! WATCHPOINTS**
Use eggs at room temperature, not straight from the refrigerator. Cold egg whites do not give as great a volume when whisked. Take great care when separating the whites from the yolks; any trace of yolk will prevent the white from foaming.

**✳ FREEZING**
The Lemon Pavlova freezes well. Preferably the meringue case should be made in a 22 cm/8½ inch foil plate, not on a sheet of paper. Fill the meringue case and open freeze before placing in a large rigid container. Alternatively, the meringue case can be frozen unfilled, then defrosted at room temperature for about 1 hour and filled when ready to serve. Lemon Pavlova, filled and un-filled, can be stored for up to 2 months in the freezer.

●320 calories/1350 kj per portion

## MAKING MERINGUE CASE AND LEMON FILLING

**1** *Whisk the egg whites until they are stiff enough to stay in position if the bowl is turned upside down.*

**2** *Spread meringue evenly over circle of paper and spoon or pipe the rest to form the sides.*

**3** *The lemon mixture is ready when it will slide cleanly straight from the spoon without trickling.*

# INDEX

**Picture Credits**

Theo Bergstrom: 86, 95
Martin Brigdale: 12, 18, 82, 93,
    103
Paul Bussell: 16
Alan Duns: 8, 30, 97, 99, 100, 114
James Jackson: 7, 17, 21, 28, 33,
    52, 58, 59, 61, 76, 80, 107, 109
Michael Kay: 62
Chris Knaggs: 73
Bob Komar: 56, 57
Don Last: 23, 27, 41, 88
Fred Mancini: 42, 55, 79, 104
Peter Myers: 25, 48, 68, 117
Roger Phillips: 45, 46, 84, 91
Paul Webster: 15, 34, 35, 37, 39,
    50, 64, 66, 71, 75, 110, 113
Paul Williams: 11
Graham Young: 119